THE REP TEXAS

TEXAS' LAST STAND FOR FAITH AND FREEDOM

To: Tina + Joseh
Fly Inverted

Gary Bray

GARY BRAY

503-349-1113

The Republic of Texas: Texas' Last Stand for Faith and Freedom

Trilogy Christian Publishers
A Wholly Owned Subsidary of Trinity Broadcasting Network
2442 Michelle Drive, Tustin, CA 92780

For information about special discounts for bulk purchases, please contact Trilogy Christian Publishing.

Manufactured in the United States of America
10 9 8 7 6 5 4 3 2 1
Library of Congress Cataloging-in-Publication Data is available.

ISBN: 978-1-68556-390-5
E-ISBN: 978-1-68556-391-2

DEDICATION

This book is dedicated to the Lord Jesus Christ, who it is written for and inspired by as a view of what a society worshiping Him would look like. It is secondly dedicated to my wife, Marilyn, and son, Brandon, to whom my life is forever owed.

This book is written for Christians and free-market believers who would like to see what a country they were governed with those two principles lifted up. This book affirms their beliefs and paints a picture of what the country would look like if you turned everything over to God. Finally, it is for anyone who would like to understand how economics would work if it were allowed to expand naturally without government interference working as an ally rather than a protagonist.

TABLE OF CONTENTS

INTRODUCTION

Steven Moses stepped out of his Black Stallion hover jet wearing his dress khaki slacks and cowboy boots as the hot Texas wind whipped him across the face. That South wind brings not only a sweltering marine humidity but a heat that cooks you to the core. Steven was a tall man with muscular, chiseled looks, the kind you get from years of hard work in the oil fields. He grew up as a rigger, where he was well known for working hard and playing even harder in his early years. His well-trimmed beard looked as good on his wildcatter rigs as it did in the boardroom in his Wrangler suit and boots.

Women noticed him immediately with his thick, blondish brown hair and the way he filled out his shirts with his barrel chest and wide shoulders from years of wrestling pipe in the Texas oil patch. Most folks were drawn to him being the most powerful man in Texas, making him the richest man in the world. Steven has been married to his job ever since his wife Sandy succumbed to cancer seven years ago. He still wore his wedding ring to remind himself of their years together and to deal with the pain he still felt in his heart.

The turn of the century seems like an eternity ago, he thought. *We had the rise of the markets, the attack on the towers, and the recession, followed by the 2025 depression, which led to Texas seceding from the Union and declaring its sovereignty. Now Texas, in six short years, has grown into the most powerful country on the planet, with Moses Oil and its conglomerates proudly standing as the largest company in Texas. Sandy would never believe what had happened.*

Steven Moses grew up in the oil patch as a third-generation wildcatter. His dad and grandfather never made much money, but they did what they loved: gambling on oil wells. Sandy Sanderson was his high-school first love, and they married after he graduated from Texas Tech with honors in Engineering. They were married for eight years before she found the lump in her breast, which was malignant. It slowly tore her away from him. He never loved anybody else and simply married his work and research, which is why he kept wearing his wedding ring.

His research had led him to a patent on a chemical compound that thins oil ten thousand feet underground, allowing companies like his to reclaim old dry wells. Oil wells before Moses' additives were only able to profitably pump half of what was in the reservoir. They were then abandoned as they began to drill down to another reservoir and then another. After he invented the Moses additive, it was like pumping free oil. Steven would buy the abandoned wells for pennies on the dollar. Then with his additives, they once again became productive, and oil was easy to produce without having to drill, making him and everyone around him very wealthy people.

When the great collapse happened, it bankrupted almost every state in the old United States and especially those with spending out of control like New York, Maryland, and California, making for tough times for their citizens and businesses. America was so desperate financially that when Texas voted and offered to buy their way out of the union, the rest of the states jumped at the chance. The Texas Succession Bill passed the US Congress in a couple of months and was signed by the President to form the Republic of Texas—a country built on cheap energy and free and unfettered energy markets. It was a chance Texans were willing to take.

Flying in from Platform 452 was uneventful; however, entering the Houston airways was always a touchy adventure. He thought it seemed like everybody in Texas owned a hover jet, and they were always coming or going from Houston, even at this hour in the morning, which kept you on your stick. The Moses Tower stood out like a Lone Star sentinel in this energy capital. It was the tallest skyscraper in America, standing as a monument to energy and free markets, and it was shaped like the biggest oil rig in the world. The crosswinds and downdrafts were tricky at twenty-three hundred fifty feet where his landing platform was located. He approached from the south and squared her up, crabbing into a perfect three-point touchdown.

Flying was Steven's favorite hobby when he wasn't working. It allowed him a chance to clear his mind from the stress of being the leader of this conglomerate. Danny, the air porter, gave him a friendly, "Good morning! And God bless you, Steven!" as he rolled the new beauty to the executive hanger. As Steven walked into the 230th floor of Moses Oil Corporation, the express elevator whisked him to his top-floor suite, and he was met by his personal secretary, Debra Jenkins.

"Good morning, Steven. President Stewart has been calling you all morning to find out about our negotiations with China and how much oil you think we can send them. Why haven't you been answering your earplug?"

"Easy, Debra, I was taking the new hover jet for a spin over the Gulf and really didn't want to take my mind off my enjoyment. If you weren't married or I wasn't single, I would swear you were my wife with your constant need to know where and what I'm doing."

"You will never let a girl get close enough to have a chance!" She giggled at their favorite joke. Debra was the type of girl who was just as pretty in a tailored suit and makeup as she was in blue jeans and no makeup in a very country, feminine way. She could have been a Cowboys' cheerleader with her attractive farm-girl face and wavy, shoulder-length copper-red hair. She was wearing a flowery green dress suit, which hugged her curves modestly but smartly.

She grew up in Longview, Texas, on a wheat farm and was at the top of her high school class, then graduated A&M with honors in business management. All the boys wanted to take her out, but she had a sweet spot for awkward, geeky guys. When she met Dan Jenkins at a college church retreat, she melted. He was from Houston, and while they were playing volleyball, it was obvious he was not very athletic. When Dan got tangled in the net and fell in a heap, she giggled, turning him five shades of red, which she found so cute, opening the door to her heart.

Dan was studying chemistry and engineering at A&M, and when he graduated *summa cum laude*, they married. Now, seven years and three babies later, they were still crazy in love. Dan worked as a head engineer at Texas Air Company, producing long-range, high-speed courier drones. They were living a dream life with Debra's parents staying with them in their retirement and helping to watch little Davey, Bobby, and Sandra. Debra would love to be a full-time mom, but the money at Moses Oil was great and hours flexible, so she stayed in one of the best jobs in the world.

"Call it my female need to know everything. I'll get President Stewart on the line for you if you are ready. Oh, and don't forget, you have a lecture this afternoon at the University of Texas up in Austin."

"Don't remind me! You know how I hate giving these boring lectures to a bunch of uninterested students on how I made lemons into lemonade. Not to mention their being journalism students who will be grilling me about everything except how this works. Give me five minutes to get the files we'll need and then put him in the virtual imaging chair, and would you send Drake in, please?"

"Did I hear my name?" Jeff Drake walked in, who was the CFO of Moses Oil. "What does that new bird do, around six-fifty? Seven hundred? Bet it turns on a dime! Can't wait until we go checking out some platforms! I saw you coming in on the roof and knew you wanted to go over the Chinese proposal while you talked with President Stewart. Listen, these Chinese, as always, are trying to drive a tight bargain into the future. They're demanding we supply them before the Koreans or Australians. We must find a way to keep everybody happy while not stretching ourselves too thin on contracts. You know they would be more than happy to continue to dominate the Asian energy markets as well as put a headlock on Taiwan. Then, of course, there is the triangle of them selling their bonds to us while lending to the US, which is a bit touchy financially."

President Stewart's image appeared on the virtual chair with a big, "Hello! Help me out, Steven. Tell me you can keep everybody satisfied

The Republic of Texas

and my neck out of the noose. Seems that becoming the world's leading producers of NatGas and refined oil products is making us very popular, although it is starting to put us in a vice."

"Sorry, Mr. President, but we're just getting Refinery 17 on the line here in a couple of months. We're buying raw crude from wherever we can get it. Our problem is with prices going up as strong as they are, we're not able to hit the targets necessary to fill their orders at a profit. Of course, we're buying futures to offset the higher-priced tankers we're buying on the cash markets. In addition, we expect to receive more oil from our own production as it is developed. The moderate prices in the shale production from the western United States help, but we could use a hundred tankers rather than the seventy-five available on the spot markets. The good news is once these tankers are processed, we should be able to bring on some more of our production as our new Gulf deep wells start producing.

"Are you still getting grief from DC wanting us to loan them more money?"

"Of course!" President Stewart mocked. "I told them as long as they continue as a socialist country and spend money without any fiscal considerations, they can buy our energy and fuels, but don't expect us to finance their spending programs."

Jeff answered, "This is going to be a balancing act with these countries as they continue to go down the path toward their spiraling financial disaster. Until they bring real fiscal responsibility to the table, they are going to continue to live hand-to-mouth. For the time being, we will play at these levels, but in the future, we'll need to rein them in a bit."

"Thanks for your time, David. Drake and I have a meeting down in Austin, and I have a speech to some students at the university to give. We'll be seeing you later today."

The corporate shuttle to Austin was uneventful, although the checkerboard of Texas farmlands and ranches never gets boring. Steven and Drake met Professor June Darling at her office as they were greeted by Dean Sherwood of the Journalism School with a refreshing cup of coffee. June Darling was an attractive woman who was friendly in a scattered sort of way. She had deep green eyes, which looked like round emeralds the way the sunlight reflected off them. Her strawberry blonde hair had a lazy curl which was pulled into a ponytail that cascaded just past her thin shoulders. She was wearing a pink flowered sundress, which showed off her attractive shape but was very conservative in a girlish style. She was trans-minding into her goggle screen, deep in thought as she was still intuitive writing when they walked in.

Dean Sherwood did the introductions. "Professor Darling, this is Steven Moses and Jeff Drake. Mr. Moses, Mr. Drake, this is June Darling."

"Oh, excuse me! I was just trying to get this article finished before I introduced you to the students. Mr. Moses and Mr. Drake, I am so honored to meet you both, and the kids are thrilled you would take the time to come to talk to them."

"My pleasure, ma'am. I hope they're not going to be too tough on me!" He thought she was more excited than he expected on a campus, but then, these schools are not like the ones in other countries. Her office was neat and clean, with screens lining the top of her walls, allowing her to monitor events as they happened around the world.

"Well, we shall see," she teased, leading Steven to the large auditorium.

They walked through a side door, and she went to the front of the auditorium to the main lectern. Her small frame was dwarfed by the size of the room, with over a thousand students filling every chair while the back was three-deep with students lining the walls. There was a full bank of remote cameras feeding home universities and web-motes for thousands streaming in around the country.

"Hello, everybody! We are so glad to have you here and honored to have one of the true pioneers of industry from our Lone Star Republic.

Mr. Steven Moses is here as our special guest, and we would ask that you allow him to give an opening statement before we begin a question-and-answer session for the next ninety minutes. As you all know, he is the CEO of Moses Enterprises and its conglomerates, an innovator and pioneer who has had incredible success in the energy sector. So, without any further ado, it is my great pleasure to introduce to the University of Texas Journalism School, Mr. Steven Moses!"

As he walked to the middle of the floor, a thunderous applause came up from the crowd as they stood up in unison to give him a standing ovation. He looked around the auditorium at the young faces, all smiling and nodding with a few approving shouts as they continued their applause.

He finally signaled them to be seated and thanked them for their warm welcome. Steven didn't expect such a rock star welcome or to have to humbly ask them to sit down to start.

"First of all, I would like to thank God who has been with me and my family to help me through both the tough times as well as the good. Some may look at me in envy, but being successful in many ways is tougher than being broke since so many more people depend on you. I have thousands of people working for me, so if I fail, thousands of people's lives are turned upside down—just like happened to me when I was running my own small company. Only back then, nobody knew me or cared how I did. As most of you know, when the United States collapsed, Texas was the only state left solvent financially. We didn't want to become bankrupt like the rest of the union, which is why we filed for secession and purchased our way into sovereignty and freedom.

"We then instituted the identical constitution as the United States, which ensured this would become a capitalist country based on free trade and individual rights, both economically and individually. These principles value small government and low taxes, which led to one of the greatest economic miracles in the history of the world. Texas has become the number one economy built on energy, which was a natural fit with our reconstituted wells along with the development of the hybrid turbo natural gas engine. This developed into the Texas Ford NatGas auto industry, and the rest is history. Texas is not only the energy capital of the world but also exports more cars and flying vehicles than any other country.

"Energy is not only the lifeblood of our country. It's also the building block for our economy as it provides a cost-effective, solid foundation upon which we built every other industry. An abundant, low-cost energy resource gives us a price-competitive edge in the worldwide marketplace since, in reality, energy costs are the building blocks of everything you make or use. Energy costs are the main expense of every product and are reflected in both transportation and manufacturing. If you can control and lower your energy costs, you will lower your production cost for everything else, which is what has made us the free-market economic power we have become.

"As we developed one market, such as our NatGas vehicles, it naturally led us into the hover jet industry and all the engineering and aerospace transportation avenues, which just spontaneously emerged. That is the beauty of this capitalistic free market system we have here in Texas. Our industries have no government interference or needless restrictions, allowing people to research and develop the products and the marketplace demands, which then allows you to always be on the cutting edge of product evolution. Those are the basics of how the Texas miracle happened, and now I will answer your questions."

Professor Darling asked the first question, "Mr. Moses, what is it that makes Texas and the free market such a powerful economic engine so that it dwarfs other economies like the US, Europe, and China?"

He thought her hair looked stunning pulled back in that ponytail but would look better down around her feminine shoulders and wearing cowboy boots, although those sandals looked really good on her with the red toenails…what?

"Well, our economy…and please, call me Steven, Professor Darling. Mr. Moses sounds too biblical." He enjoyed how his flirtatious tone turned her a nice crimson rouge in front of her students.

He let the laughter die down to answer the question. "Seriously, capitalism is the natural basis of mankind which allows us to reach our full potential. Capitalism maximizes the individual's freedom and flexibility so folks can test and expand the limits of their abilities. It is the only economic system ever invented which rewards a person for exactly what they are worth, man or woman. It is by far the most efficient transfer of goods and services ever devised by mankind."

He continued, "Capitalism allows the free flow of ideas to maximize the limits of our possibilities. Rather than having governments make every decision and determining what is good and bad, it allows the free market to decide the value in real-time from one market to another. Capitalism is the ultimate open market, just like you see in the old movies where people haggle over every purchase, but it moves that open market worldwide and in every transaction twenty-four-seven, three-sixty-five. For example, a year ago, due to our abundance of natural gas as a by-product of our production of oil products, we had a cheap source of energy to produce electricity with our NatGas electrical plants.

"An aluminum company called me from China and asked what kind of program we could put together from our electrical generation. He told me where I had to price this energy to make him come to Houston. Not only did we meet that target, but we beat it by ten percent by transferring some of our excess production to the building of another NatGas plant, which we were planning on building a bit later anyway. So now they are making more money and keeping it while hiring another five hundred workers from the Houston area. It's a natural symbiotic relationship as it is meant to work without government interference.

"When you take the government and regulators out of the equation, it makes the negotiations more efficient. We were able to put this transaction together in a matter of days rather than the months or years it takes a government having decisions fluctuating up and down the chain of authority."

"Thank you, Mr....er...Steven," blushed Professor Darling. "We're going to our question-and-answer session now. Justice," she said, pointing to the black student in the front of the line of questioners.

"Mr. Moses, sir, my name is Justice Thompson. I grew up in the District of Columbia and would just like to thank you for all you have done for young men like me. I immigrated to Texas three years ago and just completed the work and reeducation program six months ago, and thank God every day I'm here. I was raised in a family that loved the American system with all the free programs, but I grew up reading about capitalism and free markets. So, when Texas seceded, I knew I wanted to come here and experience what true freedom would be like. I am so honored to meet you face-to-face since you represent everything right in the world. God bless you.

"You helped sponsor me through the First Baptist Church of Houston where I stayed and worked for the Texas Ford Engineering Department learning about the free market, and everything you said is right. I am now working nights and going to school during the days to be a journalist and write the truth about how great this Republic of Texas is. I am starved for the truth, and I know millions of young people like me are, too, so I want to be able to explain the free market to them. So, thank you, and my question is, why don't other countries follow our church welfare program, and could you explain it to the students here that may not know what it is or how it works?"

"Well, you're welcome, Justice, and you are the reason we have those programs. We have a very tight immigration system since we are surrounded by states full of people who would love to come here with our two percent unemployment rate as well as high wages and low taxes, meaning more take-home pay or more freedom. We allow a half million people per year to immigrate, but with the understanding, they want to become capitalists in every sense of the word, who believe in freedom *of* religion, not freedom *from* religion, and who are willing to dedicate three to five years of their lives to become Texas citizens.

"Most come with nothing but the clothes on their backs, so we plug them into one of the numerous churches we have in the state immediately. We found the churches work better than the government to provide food and shelter with all their free volunteers. We call it "one-stop welfare," where they are not only fed physically but mentally and spiritually as well. Meanwhile, they go to the training schools to help them begin to reeducate themselves with economic and social classes about free markets and why they work. You would be amazed how many do not know the slightest thing about the benefits of living in a free-market economy. All they know are the risks of failure rather than any opportunities of success. Outsiders call it brainwashing, but we call it reversing their previous brainwashing, and people like Justice Thompson are free to leave if they want, but most find it to be the best thing they have ever done. Am I right, Justice?"

"Amen, Mr. Moses! It has been the best education of my life since I was starved to hear the truth about capitalism. It freed my mind to think, and I'm excited to get my degree and become a self-published journalist. Maybe I will write your story. Do you need a biographer??" The entire auditorium rang out with laughter.

The next student in line was a young woman whose name was Michelle Davis. "Mr. Moses, how do you make sure that business and government are not filled with corruption such as we see in other countries—like the United States?"

"That is a great question, Ms. Davis, and goes to the heart of why capitalism works. First, you must have honest people with integrity making the decisions since there are so many opportunities for corruption. You must trust everyone involved. It comes down to the old saying that you need to work with people who will do the right thing when no one is watching. If you are not, you will have to always be watching everyone all the time, which costs money.

"It helps that we are a Christian nation in that people know the difference between right and wrong, or telling the truth and lying. It is no coincidence we are the most Christian nation in the world, with eighty percent going to and being involved with Christian-based churches in Texas. It is also no coincidence we have the lowest crime rate in the world as well as divorce and drug addiction rates. We value God, the family, and private property, so people value other people's possessions and freedom.

"The second part about government corruption is how you and our computerized system come in. We have complete transparency in all our industries. If you are doing the right thing, you have nothing to hide. Of course, some of it is sensitive and cannot be shared, but we want everything and everyone to share their knowledge with the public. This is where you budding journalists fit in, and we want you to report the story, both good and bad. Write your critical articles, but have the same vigor and passion for reporting what is going right since nearly all the businesses are honest, although you never hear about them."

The next question was from a boy who looked like he was a football player. He was tall and wide with not an ounce of fat on him, and his cowboy hat only made him look like a horse on two legs. "Mr. Moses, my name is Tom Johnson. I was recruited out of Chicago to play defensive line for the Longhorns and am trying to immigrate—if you can get me some help? My question is, being from Chicago, how did you keep the unions out and from messing everything up, and why does nobody want an hourly wage?"

"Well, son, I don't have that kind of clout to get your citizenship, but you may want to talk to Coach Brown, Jr. Most think he has more clout than President Stewart in Texas! That's a good question, Tom. The short answer is nobody wants the unions. The long answer is, every time they come down here, they find out they cannot match piecework. Once we computerized our wages, we had real-time wage negotiations and could work out a salary as the worker improved his value to the company. This evolved into piecework, and the value inputs were invented, and matrices were formed to pay someone for every job he did. Whether it was turning screws or keying in contracts, it all came down to activities the computer could track and value by the second, which is far more than the hourly rate could pay. The employee became his own business by being the controller of his paycheck.

"The advantage is, it encourages the workers to work harder, smarter, and more efficiently, making the companies more productive. This is how we are bringing business from China and other low-wage countries since our workers are motivated and passionate about their work and their companies. They essentially share in the success of the company by making the company even more successful. We have a saying at Moses Oil: 'You are the key, and we are your doorway.' It means we all work together to unlock success. That is how the free market works."

"Hello, Mr. Moses. I, too, am proud to have you here. You are a hero in my family. My name is Miguel Martinez, and my family has lived in Texas for five generations. I was fourteen when the Texas secession happened. Could you explain how and why it did?"

Steven was moved by the statement and caught himself thinking about those events. "Miguel, it was a long process moving away from the United States. As you may know, we were a very patriotic state and loved the American ideal, but the federal government became so overbearing and regulatory that it was destroying our economy and our state. When America became so overextended financially and collapsed, there was an overabundance of pain and suffering, especially in the major cities. They wanted to take more taxes from us since we were still producing oil for the rest of America and the world. We were one of the only states still operating with a positive budget due to being fiscally conservative in addition to working with our church partnerships.

"We tried to fight it in Congress, but they wouldn't listen. In fact, since we were so outnumbered and outvoted, they doubled the taxes they were taking from us since we were an oil-producing state. The final straw was passing new regulations which were going to shut down our oil industries, so we really had no choices. We drew up our own Declaration of Independence and submitted it to the President of the United States. That's when Congress declared war on Texas and ordered all our offices seized by the National Guard.

"When the Texas Minutemen gathered, a few other prominent businessmen and I combined our resources and offered the US fifty trillion dollars for our independence. Then-US President Sanchez thought we were crazy, but when he saw the names on the declaration and which companies were leveraging their finances, he realized we could actually pay the bill. He then took it to Congress.

"Congress had me speak as the leader of the coalition, and I explained to them that not only could we pay the money but would guarantee them energy for the following decade at a reduced rate so long as they would not take military actions against us. We enjoyed a lot of help from our senators and congressmen who guided our Declaration through Congress. At that point, there was really nothing they could say or do since they knew there would be an ugly war between the states, and we had all the guns and troops we needed. So, they debated a couple of months and gave us our sovereignty with a few caveats, and now here we are!

"Not only did we pay them off ahead of the scheduled terms, but we also have grown so fast that we have expanded ten times the rate we were growing as a state. This has been an amazing adventure both as a country and as an industry. We are proving to the world what can happen if a country and the free market work together rather than as antagonists. Thanks be to God for all these events and for bringing such a fine team together. I passionately believe this was an act of the Holy Spirit to free Texas and its people from the oppression we see in the US today."

Professor Darling stood and walked forward, addressing the crowd, "That is all the time we have. Ah, Steven, and we would certainly like to—"

One of the boys in the back yelled, "Don't mess with Texas!" And the entire audience stood in applause and cheering like they had just beaten the Aggies. The chant went on for over five minutes while both Steven and Professor Darling tried to settle them down.

Steven Moses regained himself and finished by saying, "Thank you so much for your attendance, your patriotism, and your enthusiasm, which only encourages me that we have another generation of Texans who will build on what we have started. Make sure to study hard, work hard, and pray hard, for tomorrow will be here before you know it. Everybody now, may God bless Texas!"

As they walked back to her office, they enjoyed the warm sun highlighting the beauty of the campus with all the deep green grass and multiple varieties of trees and flowers. He could hear a turtledove cooing in a dogwood tree across the campus. He could smell a slight hint of honeysuckle wafting through the air, adding sweetness to the warm, humid Gulf breeze.

"Thank you so much for coming and speaking to our school, Mr. Moses. It was such an interesting speech. The students enjoyed your talk, which was so inspirational for them to hear. You are very generous with your time, and we appreciate how valuable it is."

Such an intriguing woman, Steven thought. *Very pretty, yet in a bit of a plain sort of way.* She carries an air of being hurt by a man at some point, and if he guessed, it would be in the past year or so, which is why she seemed so distant.

"How long have you been teaching at Texas?" he quizzed as they arrived at her small office in the Bush Building.

"I have been a professor here for two years and have been a virtual author for the *Austin Gazette Online* for much of that time. Before then, I was studying to earn my doctorate while I wrote for both *The New York Times* and *The Washington Post* as a syndicated writer."

"Should I consider you the enemy, Professor Darling?"

"Oh, hardly! I was the lone free marketer at those papers and was considered a *persona non grata*, but they couldn't find anyone else to write for them. In fact, I covered much of the secession and Declaration of Independence. I actually interviewed you via e-mail as a graduate student."

"Well, anytime you want to interview me again, it would be my pleasure. Would you like to get a cup of coffee? Is there a good spot around here, Professor Darling?"

"Oh, ah, well, Mr. Moses, I really can't. I mean, I'm not really ready to begin any relationship or anything. Besides, I am kind of seeing someone and—"

"Look, I ain't asking you to marry me or anything! I just thought you might want to talk over a cup of coffee. Why is it every pretty woman immediately thinks if you want to talk, you want to get married? And my name is Steven; can I call you June?"

June began fidgeting with her ponytail. "Well, no, I mean, yes…ah, no, I didn't think you were asking to marry me. What? Yes, June is fine; and there is a nice little cafe across the commons for coffee." *Where did that come from? You sound like a babbling fool,* she thought.

They both laughed at the moment as she grabbed her purse and jacket. "I would be interested in interviewing you some time when you have an hour about a project I'm working on."

"Well, sure, that would be fine, although you may find my life is far more boring than you think."

"How can your life be boring? You're one of the richest, most powerful men in the world! You probably have beautiful women throwing themselves at you."

They walked into a crowded little cafe called The Longhorn Bistro and Brew. It was crowded with students who were enjoying good food and coffee, as well as the older students having the cold beer and burger combination. Country Western music was playing in the background, making for a real Texas flavor.

"Why should you worry if women throw themselves at me?"

"Oh, ah…I don't. I was just stating the obvious." She knew she said something she should not have, *but he is handsome,* she thought. She tried to make herself stop thinking that. She was still getting over Tom, who had been the dream of her life, until he ran off with one of his students. *Men are such creeps.*

"What is obvious?" He was teasing her now.

"What? Oh, well, you know, you are rich and powerful. You are a very good catch for most women. Oh, brother, how do I get out of this, and is there a way out?" They both laughed at her three shades of red.

"So, June, not to change the subject, but did you grow up here? And where is your family?"

"I grew up in Tyler, Texas, where my dad is a pastor at a small church, Trinity Baptist. He is the pastor, and my mom plays the piano and sings. Trinity had around 150 members and was a really small community. I have two brothers and a sister who are very close. I love Texas and the university. Are you also close with your parents?"

"Yes. My dad, William, has always been my inspiration. He showed me how to live my life. My mom, Katherine, is the best mother a kid could want. She really kept the family together while my dad was out drilling in the Gulf or in some Texas jackrabbit gulch. She just loved all of us and made a perfect home. When Dad came home, it was like Christmas. He was gone weeks at a time and sometimes months out of the country. He would always come home with a bag of candy to make it festive. He worked hard and kept us safe and secure."

"Did you miss him while he was gone?"

"Of course, and he missed lots of baseball and basketball games. All the other kids' dads were the same. They worked in the Gulf, too, so we all got used to it. It was just part of growing up, but when I got old enough to work in the fields, he was my best friend and mentor, showing me the ropes. He became the best dad a guy could ever hope for to learn the important parts of life."

"Why haven't you remarried or have a wife and family?"

He laughed off the pain that question always brought in his chest. "Is that a proposal?"

"Stop it, I'm not that kind of girl," she said, laughing. She sensed the hurt he still felt from his wife's death. "Did your parents take you to church? Are you religious?"

"Yes, I accepted Christ as a young boy at church camp. We went to Calvary Foursquare growing up, but I strayed for a while—you know, sowing my oats. When Sally died, I became angry at God for what he did to me and for punishing her with such a horrible death. I thought God was a cold and punishing God, and He liked bringing innocent people like Sally such pain. In the end, it made me stronger, and I realized I could love someone with all my heart and soul. Even though losing her hurts, we still are together, which is why I am still single. Fortunately, I had a friend on an oil rig who was a Christian, and as we talked, I rededicated my heart to Jesus. I don't know what I would do without Him. He is my entire life now."

She looked at the wedding ring he still wore. "Is that why you still wear your wedding ring? Because of the pain?"

"Oh, that, yes. I had never been hurt like that in my life when I lost Sandy. For the first year, it felt like my heart had been pulled out of my chest and stomped on. She saved me from a life of drinking and fighting and turned it around. She was the perfect woman for me, and I don't think there can be anyone to fill that scar in my chest. It also lets women know I am off-limits since I'm really married to my career and company anyway. Pretty much a stop sign on my hand. Kind of sad, huh?"

"No, not at all. She was a lucky woman to have a man so dedicated to her to still consider himself married after her death. It's charming."

"As for the 'no wife and family,' all I can say is, I am a workaholic, and I wouldn't want to raise my kids the way I was raised. If I were to have a family, I would have to give up most of my work, and I really enjoy my work. What about you? Do you love your job?"

"Oh, absolutely, this is the best career in the world! There are very few places you can help to teach kids not only how to report the news but also to explain how it affects their lives. Very few people really understood it when we first left the States, so it was our job to teach our journalists how economies work and retrain them to write about the wonders of capitalism and freedom. That is our job and my calling. We are pioneers in a field that was designed to take businesses down and promote an agenda. We are the new reporters who are fighting the war of words to lift-up free markets and explain how they empower the individual spirit through entrepreneurship and creativity. Most do not understand a business is really an individual. It is simply an individual entity representing a group of people with a common goal speaking as one voice."

"Now I am in love." Steven teased as June playfully slapped his hand when his phone rang. "Yes, hello. Drake? How was President Stewart? Yeah, it is getting hectic. We are at the Longhorn Bistro and Brew; why don't you come over?"

"What?"

"Now?"

"I can't…really?"

"Okay, I'll be there in a few minutes."

He hung up and looked at June, rolling his eyes. "Now you know why I never remarried. Apparently, I'm needed at President Stewart's office to work something out. I'm not sure what it is, but it sounds like something to do with the new proposals by the United Nations. Can I walk you back to your office before I head over there?"

"No, that's not necessary. I must stop by the library first and then a couple of other things I need to do. It was a pleasure. And thank you so much for talking to my students. They enjoyed it so much."

"Can I see you again, and perhaps you can have that real interview."

"Perhaps an interview, but the time just isn't right for either of us," she said, wondering if she was passing up something she had been waiting for or was he more trouble than she needed right now. She didn't want to get hurt again, and besides, her new boyfriend David was hinting at getting married. Oh, why now?

Steven looked into her eyes and said, "Like my dad always told me, 'Never wait for the next cab when the one you may need is parked right in front of you.' I will let you know when we can do the interview." Steven looked into those sparkling green eyes, feeling them tug him in as his mind swam around in their reflective deep green pools of life. "I better get going, and it was very nice meeting you, Professor Darling."

He shook her hand and turned to go, heading for his shuttle over to the capital.

A STORM IS BREWING

United Nations Secretary-General Salinas Margarita Polentas looked out her office down at New York City. She could remember when she first arrived at the UN as an assistant for the Venezuelan ambassador. In those days before the US collapse, you could walk around the city without having to worry about your safety, which she took full of advantage of and searched every corner of New York. Sure, there were places in the city you would not want to be out after dark, but not like now.

The rampant gangs and mafia have turned the UN blocks into an armed compound you never leave except by air, and even then, you may get shot at by a laser or missile. You wouldn't want to end up like the bloody bodies she saw this morning hanging from a lamppost with a "Banker" sign attached to his chest. On the next post was a woman with "Stockbroker" attached to hers. Then, of course, there were the human crosses. It was too gruesome to think what a horrible death they must have faced until hanging became a welcome escape.

The city has turned into complete anarchy as entire sections are "every man for himself," being completely taken over by the gangs. For a woman like herself, to be out after dark was a chilling thought. The only areas that were safe were the walled sections of the Upper East Side, some of the villages, and East Long Island, which had become armed compounds with everyone working from home and not letting anybody into their cities which doesn't have proper ID. Unless there were natural defenses, the city had fallen into complete chaos.

There were no cars in the city as nobody could afford gas even if they had the proper rationing chips. The streets were empty since everyone took the subway. It has become not only the transportation hub, but the tunnels were also the underground-economy centers of the cities. Everything from fuel to people was traded down there, out of the way of the police and authorities who could never patrol the labyrinth of tunnels.

Looking out over the dead city, you could see the skyscrapers with missing windows. The electricity only worked periodically since coal had been outlawed, and nuclear-powered plants shuttered while renewable sources were unreliable even when they were maintained. This has made the rail and subways only able to work on occasion, not that anybody would want to go down there to be robbed or raped during blackouts. When trains shut down, the people on board were free game for the gangs.

There is only one answer to this problem, Secretary Polentas thought, *and that was to have Texas provide America with cheaper electricity and begin paying taxes like every other country in the world. It was not fair that they should have all their excessive wealth when so many people were suffering from hunger and poverty around the world. There was just so much good she and the UN could do; if the Texans would just pay their fair share, they could solve those problems. It was not right that a country should be so wealthy and not help the world pull itself out of this worldwide depression.*

The citizens were becoming ungovernable ever since the collapse. Sure, they were paying seventy percent taxes, which was hard, but the UN and America needed more revenue to provide the services the people required. Why didn't they understand the simple fact that we were doing what we could to keep the people from starving on the four corners of the world? She thought about the never-ending sirens and lights keeping her up during the night. Sure, she was safe in the UN condos inside the complex, but it would be great to get a decent night's sleep without the yelling, the screams, and the sirens; guess that is the price of living in the Big Apple. If something didn't change soon, this city could destroy itself, turning it into mass riots like it had never seen before.

Her Chief of Staff entered her office, snapping her out of her thoughts.

"Secretary-General, the United States President is here. The Security Council has been assembled, and both are waiting for you in the board-room."

She took the short walk to the elevators and down to the inner board-room where the ten economic leaders were waiting: the UN ambassadors of the United States and the President, the ambassadors to China, Russia, Japan, Chile, Saudi Arabia, Iraq, Germany, and Britain.

She opened the meeting, "Thank you, ladies and gentlemen, for coming, and especially President Chambers. You all know why we are here. We have written and are going to propose to the General Assembly UN Measure 2033–311, which will require any country that wants to import or export to a UN member country will have to be a full-paying member of the UN. This, of course, will require all our countries to have equal footing with other countries. They will come under the UN Charter for fair and equitable trading practices. This will generate more business for every country and stop any one country from exploiting other less advanced countries through inequitable trade practices. Questions? President Chambers, you have a question?"

President Chambers was the newly elected president from Boston and came out of its Socialist Party machine. He was an ardent fighter for the nationalized health care and social programs, then was a supporter to maintain the programs the United States had developed over the past century. He came from a hardworking family whose father owned a small grocery store in north Boston. The family knew everybody, and his father was well connected in the Democrat Party until it morphed into the Socialist Party as the Republican Party simply imploded into the Constitutional Party. His rise in party politics was dramatic. He went from State Representative to Governor, and midway through his governorship ran for President and won. He had no idea how difficult this would be as the chronic unemployment would not stop increasing and currently was at twenty-nine percent.

"Madam Secretary and distinguished Ambassadors, you know this resolution puts us in a difficult position with the Republic of Texas. We have been allies since their secession and have stood in the way of three other of these resolutions. There are numerous issues with this proposal that will affect us in many ways. The least of which is they are our largest trading partner; we import sixty-five percent of our oil and power from them. We will need assurances from the council that we will have our energy needs covered by your member countries.

"Our other issue is their maintaining our debt by purchasing our bonds. When they originally split from America, we agreed on a price of fifty trillion dollars over ten years, which we believed would help us with our services and infrastructure, but they paid it off in two years, and we have been struggling ever since. If they were to call in our debt or not purchase our bonds, we would go into default on our payments to foreign countries, triggering another worldwide financial collapse.

"Our citizens have suffered under this worldwide recession, and they are not able to pay any more taxes. The rate they are paying now is seventy percent, and we have the wealthy paying more than ninety-five percent, so where can we increase our revenue? The worst part is we are losing our most skilled people and profitable businesses to Texas. They can pay the highest wages with the best benefits of anywhere in the world, let alone the Americas, so they are taking the cream of the cream for their own empire. They have all the best engineers and most skilled technical workers, so the rest of the world no longer can compete. With their corporate and personal tax structures, there is no way we can keep our best people staying here. The only ones who are staying are the ones who are not able to immigrate due to their stringent immigration laws.

"We still have ten percent of our successful businesses who have not left, but many of those have applied. As you know, they will not let anybody through their borders unless they are at the top of their industry and/or have a patent they can use to expand their economy, like Texas Ford. Then they have a four-year education program, which educates immigrants on their economic and government structure. After five years,

The Republic of Texas

you become a citizen with the right to vote and to run for office. If they continue to take the best people and businesses in our country and the world, how are we able to compete? We need some guarantees of revenue from the UN dues and fees. We need Texas energy to survive.

"There is no way we can enter a military battle with Texas since our history, as well as citizens, would have a problem fighting against a former state. Also, our secession agreement allows us reduced prices on all energy purchases. If they were to cut us off from our energy supplies, we would have some severe shortages and outages that could cripple our economy even further. We may be able to enter a limited conflict with them, but we would need plausible deniability to free us from any connection to this action, either militarily or politically.

"You should also be advised, Madam Secretary, that we have some information from inside Texas that they have some very technological weapons. As you know, they are one of the major suppliers of laser and digital weaponry. They are very technologically advanced. We're not sure exactly how advanced they are, but our military people believe they may have some weapons being researched, which could be very effective against most attacks. They have taken the best scientists in the world for the past eight years, so it's anybody's guess what they have developed or have on the drawing board.

"In addition, we all know they have the fastest aircraft in the world. Lone Star Air has dominated the trans-world market with their aircraft ever since they unveiled these commuter ramjet space shuttles. While most of our aircraft still take eighteen hours to get to Asia, they are making the flight in a little over two. We have heard rumors their next generation is even faster and could operate sub-atmospheric, and who knows what types of fighter weaponry they can put on those types of platforms? Ladies and gentlemen, let me say as a former countryman of Texas, be very diligent in your entering any type of shooting war with these people. We will support you in your discussions and negotiations with them as well as provide as much intelligence as we can, but you have to understand we are not in a position to enter into a battle that will force them to isolate us from their energy supplies."

"Thank you, President Chambers," snapped Secretary-General Polentas. "We understand the difficult position you are in and have no intentions of putting you at risk of Texas cutting off your energy supplies. We thank you for your information, and our intelligence has verified everything you have told us and more. They are not only the most powerful country in the world economically but have dominated technological and military development, which is why we would never want to get into a shooting war with them.

"The UN military generals have looked at the difficulties of breaching their multiple walls and defensive weapons, deciding it would be nearly impossible. They have been advancing their wall security to keep American immigrants out, so they have perfected their laser taser to the point of making it nearly impossible to get past their laser robots. They have determined they could simply upgrade those robots by installing more powerful lasers to stop anything on the land or air. Texas has become a force to be reckoned with, but we think we have a way to bring them to the table, which is why we brought you here."

Terry Thomas was flying his hover jet along the northern wall, looking out into the Oklahoma red countryside, making sure he stayed just inside the Texas border. It was bad enough he had to make sure nobody was able to breach the walls or fly into their airspace, but his night optics were acting fidgety tonight. His mind was filled with so many checklists to make sure the robots were functioning or that the Okies weren't compromising their sensors spread across the farmlands disappearing across the horizon. At night, the laser creates a visual display rivaling any light show.

He knew every one of those people walking aimlessly would give their left arm to be doing what he was doing. He was in his third year of immigration, and four years ago, he was one of those in the hobo camps who just happened to graduate number three from Annapolis and became one of the best fighter jocks in the US Navy, allowing him to immigrate with a skill. The F-22s he flew was a bit more responsive than this hover jet, but he felt his piloting skills were every bit as needed. Besides, these hovers were fun to fly with all the avionics built into the joystick.

He thought back to the first year and the changes he was being taught to counter the communal thinking and beliefs he brought with him. He laughed at the thought of how he used to believe completely in the social safety net. Here in Texas, they not only don't have one but have no need for it. When you have ninety-eight percent employment, there is no need for wasteful social programs. For those who are infirmed or handicapped, they are cared for through the churches, which are far more efficient than an uncaring bureaucracy. The Texas Christ Churches feed the soul as well as the stomach to really fix what is hurting. They call it "one-stop feeding" to bring healing to the person.

He looked across at the scattered hobo campfires and wondered what they would look like if they were run by the church rather than the government. Churches were far more effective than governments since they had huge numbers of volunteers, making the donated dollars stretch further. They had been, throughout history, the primary welfare and poverty providers, and those people would not only be fed but brought back into society and productivity. If those states were not taxing their citizens out of their homes and jobs, there would be plenty of money to tithe to the churches to feed the poor. Even though he was making a lower wage than he made as a captain in the Navy, when you factored in a fifteen percent tax rate, he could not only tithe but also give to other charities like the Veterans Hospital Fund. Overtaxing and underuse of churches and faith made all those people's lives more desperately hopeless.

He thought about his second year when he began to learn about free-market economics while doing his volunteer work at his church in their food bank. After the first two years working for Border Security Inc., he could not only clean his hover from the windshield to the tail fin into a mirror finish but could tear every one of these aircraft down and rebuild it blindfolded. Those were tough years: he had a full day's work followed by six hours of economics, history, government, constitution law, and energy conservation and development. It was fourteen hours of the most intensive instruction and physically demanding work he had done in his life, but it gave him a sense of pride he had never enjoyed before. Now he was a mere twenty-six months from becoming a full voting citizen for the Republic of Texas. Who knows, now perhaps he could start looking for a wife?

Suddenly, something caught his eye in the brush as he was flying by, so he pulled into a silent hover. Looking closer, he magnified and saw what he thought it was: a nice jackrabbit. He dove in as two of them ran into the open. They were darting back and forth between the heavy brush and trees, avoiding hawks and coyotes, but he anticipated a small opening they had to cross and squeezed the lasers, killing both instantly. The boys back at the base are going to be enjoying some rabbit stew for lunch or maybe dinner tonight.

He did a couple of outside loops with one of his patented curly cues to celebrate and saw dozens more dashing across the ground as he set his craft down to do the dirty work of cleaning and skinning these two delicious, fat beauties. Even though it was just before sunrise, it was still warm and humid in the panhandle. It was not as humid as down by Houston, but it still stays warm and muggy in the early summer, even before dawn. He made short work of the cleaning and was putting them in the cooling unit when he saw something fast coming out of the corner of his eye. A military jet screamed across the grasslands, nearly passing right over the top of him doing around twelve hundred knots coming straight out of Oklahoma, about thirty feet off the treetops with no markings or lights.

Terry jumped into his craft, fired it up, and shot straight up into the air, but there was no sign of the one that just went over the top. He flashed on his laser ops, and they picked up nothing — dead air. It couldn't be more than eighty miles out by now and should be lighting his windshield like old Times Square, but nothing. He called in to Border Command and reported what he saw and asked if they had just scoped an aircraft from Oklahoma. Nothing. He knew what he just saw and heard, but how could anybody have that good a signal diverter to counter his ops? They scrambled ten more hovers, but nobody picked up or saw anything. He thought he better get back to the base to report this and then start fixing some delicious fresh rabbit stew.

What a great day with the afternoon sun shining bright and bringing happiness to the capital, even in these tense times. Steven Moses could not get June Darling off his mind, with her reddish-blonde hair and green eyes that drew him in like a moth to a midnight lightbulb on a hot summer night. He felt a bit of aching like he had not felt since Sandy was with him. Austin was a beautiful city with its artsy culture mixed with a major campus as well as the Texas capital. The Gulf winds were coming out of the equator and knocking their shuttle around a bit, and there was dense traffic at all elevations during the short hop. They landed on the top deck of the capital and walked into the president's wing. They were ushered directly into President Stewart's office, which was filled with Drake and the finance cabinet and secretaries.

His office was on the top floor of the newly built Texas White House. It resembled the Washington White House from the outside, except it was over twice as large and far more opulent and, of course, newly built with the country, which had all the latest technological advantages. His office was expansive with an adjacent boardroom for cabinet meetings, which had walls of monitors covering the entire world to talk to different leaders. He had a row of virtual chairs in which the head of the Senate and House were sitting from their offices. His office was comfortable with couches in a semicircle facing the presidential desk. The walls were covered in deep cherry paneling with gun memorabilia displayed. His pride and joy was the Sam Houston long rifle which had passed through his family and was a museum-quality piece for its place in Texan history.

"Steven, thanks for coming; you know everybody, Vice President Chavez and my cabinet members. The reason we wanted you to join us is you know we have been getting rumblings from the United Nations that they were in negotiations to change our tax and import-export agreements. We are not sure where this is going, but they have invited us to come to New York City next month to speak to the UN Council and explain our positions regarding our production and distribution of energy. The US Ambassador is hearing they may be making a move to not only increase the world tax but to take a more active role in negotiating and writing contracts to control production and distribution. He thinks they want to make us a full member with all the taxes and regulations which go with it.

"They are going to mandate that we pay a tax, and some are indicating it may be in the thirty-five percent range. As you all know, we have refused to pay any taxes, and the United States has vetoed all the bills they have introduced to single us out. We are the wealthiest country in the world, controlling sixty percent of the energy markets worldwide, so they want to take from us to give to their socialist economies in the guise of feeding the poor. The problem we may have is the US is falling into such desperate straits they may need to take our taxes too, leaving us alone without an ally on the Security Council to veto their proposal."

Steven responded, "The reason we are the economic power in the world is that we don't have one of those socialist disasters, and we have succeeded by recognizing the ingenuity of the average person who wants to maximize his talents and abilities. We are proof that if you have a small government which gets out of the way of free enterprise, the sky is truly your limit. Now they want to impose their will on us—no way! We have to fight this with every ally we have, just like we did last year and the year before."

Vice President Chavez interjected, "You all know me—my ancestors have lived in Texas since before the Alamo. I love this land with my entire heart. I will proudly die in Texas, if need be, for my great country. What we have seen since we seceded has been the greatest success story in the history of mankind with our freeing of the human spirit as well as our outward worship of the Lord. Steven, we are meeting with the Texas governors and Congress next week and would like you to speak to them about how to fight the UN and, of course, give them a background on the international energy sector you know so well. We know this is short notice, but the President and I think you are the best person to address this issue. You know all the various countries around the world and the leaders who are pushing this tax and seizure. We are meeting next Tuesday morning here in the chambers. Would you be able to be here?"

"Of course, I will, Miguel, whatever you need of me. I will be happy to speak to the governors and fill them in on who these leaders are and what they are trying to do. Obviously, since the county governors are the local service providers, they should understand how this would affect them and why we will need their support if we are going to challenge this resolution. They have benefited both by our success in building and modernizing our infrastructure as well as receiving low-cost energy and superior road-building products. If we must start sending taxes to the UN, it will force us to lower our provisions here, which could cut into our infrastructure, which will increase costs on every one of our products."

President Stewart spoke up, "We have a uniquely close relationship with our industries. We understand they need flexibility and an understanding that we are allies and not their rulers. This has been one of the main advantages we have and is our hands-off approach, which has not only allowed them to expand, but they have expanded in a responsible manner. All our inspections, as well as their paperwork, have shown that in nearly all cases, they have not only met our requirements but always exceeded all but the most absurd requirements designed to curtail production. This has made us by far the least polluting as well as the most efficient energy producers on the planet. All of this gets to the point that we have very little real power here in the capital and will be pushing our limits just to challenge this resolution, and we have no power if they decide to push the issues.

"So, gentlemen and ladies, I don't think any of us have come this far to have some two-bit bunch of socialist dictators take away everything we have built. The last thing anybody in this room wants is to go back to what we left, and if you are like me, I will die holding onto my ancestors' freedom. What they really want to take away from us is our freedom and then enslave us into their One World Government, which they claim will end poverty. As we all know, they will only make it worse as they try to take the money from us to give to corrupt dictators they've propped up around the world. So, this is the first step in a journey that we have no idea how long or far it will go. So, thank you for coming and…Don't mess with Texas!"

"Don't mess with Texas!" they all echoed in unison.

MOSES OIL

Steven arrived in the office later than the usual 7:00 a.m., knowing it was going to be a long day filled with strategy meetings. He scheduled a board meeting to fill them in on the events that he was told about in Austin and world events that were happening on a minute-by-minute basis. The heads of Moses subsidiaries were spread around the table with their assistants behind them on their two-way computer goggles, communicating updated information to be relayed as needs arose. They could all tell by Steven's somber expression that this was going to be a long and intense meeting. He didn't waste any time.

"Board members, I am glad you could all make it and hope you are all prepared. We have the greatest threat to our companies as well as this country that we've had since our independence. I know most of you have heard through the grapevine news and rumors we are about to have a massive cost and regulatory stranglehold put on us from the United Nations. You know my thoughts on their alliance of socialist dictators, but it does not matter—they have the entire world at their disposal to pressure us, which is why we are having this emergency meeting."

"Dave, what have you heard from our customers and suppliers of oil and gas?"

David Scott was a third-generation oilman whose blood was sweet Texas crude. He has either traded or owned oil commodity companies his last twenty years, making fortunes in their distribution. He became a billionaire in the shutdown of the Alaskan pipeline when he controlled most of their outside production as oil increased ten times its value in six months until the government was forced to reopen it. After the Texas secession, he let Moses Oil acquire his company and make him the head of Oil and Gas.

"Thanks, Steven, it's everything you say and worse. Sources are saying they are being pressured by the UN and their governments to stop buying and selling with Texas until we begin paying the world taxes we have refused to pay since our founding. They are saying it was fine when we first became a republic since we had no extra income and were strapped to pay back America, but now we are the leading energy-producing country in the world, and they say we should be paying our fair share.

"Our largest crude suppliers in the Middle East are torn since they have as little use for the UN as we do, but they cannot afford to look like they are siding with us. We may be able to convince some of the smaller producers like Nigeria and Israel to continue to sell to us, but even they are getting pressure from other member countries. We are quite sure we can continue to buy from the Dakotas and Alaska, but if President Chambers and the Congress step in, it is anybody's guess.

"Sales are going to be another story. It sounds like they are going to form a coalition against us and stop buying Texas products on the open market. They have all but stopped buying our futures contracts even though, as you all know, we have been forced to discount to the limit and still no buyers in the last week. We are shipping the existing contracts, but China, Japan, and Europe have all made it clear they are going to wait until the General Assembly decides what they are going to do before they step back into the market.

"America has to buy their gasoline from us as well as refined fuels, but we have heard from inside sources that Chambers has agreed to go along with the UN and is willing to cut himself off to force us to comply. This could become the old "Mexican standoff" if they go along since it will hurt them as much as it will hurt us. Then it becomes a matter of who can hold out the longest financially. That is all we know right now, Steven. We will keep you all up to speed as events develop."

"Thanks, Dave; as you can see, this may become a very large problem for our company as we have no idea how far they are willing to push this or for how long. Sam, can you give us the report on our power generation?"

Sam Satterwhite has been with Moses Power for ten years when they purchased Texas General Power and Light, of which he was the CEO. He had moved up through the ranks of Texas General as an innovator in the electrical power generation industry. His ability to position his companies in the most efficient and cost-effective mode of electrical generation has made him legendary in the industry, although a bit of a pariah among the governments who wanted to use power as a tool against their people. He stayed with the most dependable. He shunned all the fad electrical plans like solar and wind in their early stages, preferring to stay with coal and gas. When gas was being found and developed in expanding quantities, he was building NatGas electrical plants next to the refineries using their byproduct as his primary fuel. This has made Moses Power and himself legendary in the power generation industry.

"Thanks, Steven; we don't look quite as bleak as the oil side, although I'm not going to fool you into believing we won't be affected if there is a Texas boycott. We will have plenty of NatGas from our own domestic supplies and may even see prices lower if our competitors are not purchasing from us. As far as sales go, we will be able to sell to our own markets to maintain our own plants and industries, which may or may not be cut off depending on which companies they go after. Y'all know nobody is going to stop Texans from turning on their air-conditioners in the hot summer sun!

"The big issue is we sell nearly fifty percent of our power to the United States. We feed the grid from California to New York, and if they stop buying, we will really feel the loss. The bigger question is, if we were to cut off their power, they would have no way to replace it from their lack of building power plants over the last forty years in the numbers they need. Between lack of production and their antiquated grid network losing power as it escapes from their lines, they have a critical shortage. If they had updated to coaxial or laser like we have, they would be fifty percent more efficient than they are now.

"They have regular brownouts and rolling blackouts to keep from permanent blackouts, and if we pulled the switch, they could have a major blackout, shutting down the entire nation. So, one of the issues we will need to decide is if they were to act with the UN, do we act first or wait? Our estimates are that they would have a difficult time keeping the power on if we cut their power. Then if we do, how much misery would we cause? We are doing the analysis and will report on that later, but the initial models show massive disruptions of supplies of food, power, and necessities."

"Thanks, Sam. I think everybody here hopes we never have to make that decision. Tom, what are you seeing with the steel and aluminum companies?"

Tom Summers was one of the newcomers who moved out of the Rust Belt after the secession. He was the CEO for Alcoa and walked away when he saw the writing on the wall for his industry. America was destroying its own energy production, which was going to drive energy costs above the industry's ability to pay. There was no way in the middle of a recession to pass those costs on to his customers, so bankruptcy was the most likely scenario. He, too, was a living legend in the aluminum and hybrid industries, making the production more efficient and the development of stronger, lighter products, which had revolutionized the aircraft, rocket, and hovercraft industries.

"Steven, and gentlemen, we obviously have two issues just like the rest of you, except we have a competitive market to sell into. If we lose our foreign markets in airline sales as well as hover jets, we could be forced to cut back on productions. Right now, we have a market that is purchasing nearly everything we can produce, thanks to our quality and superior technology. The Asian producers have forced the markets down due to lower labor and raw material costs and have flooded the markets to some extent. The US producers have fallen so far behind in technology, thanks to the union takeover as well as their energy disadvantage; they are basically an industrial mess. The European producers have had so many shutdowns and missed deadlines that the major airlines are afraid to purchase their products for fear of never receiving shipment.

That said, the UN could force them to boycott us, and they would have to buy elsewhere.

"Our other problem will be the availability of rare minerals from around the world. As you all know, we have an advantage of abundant and cost-effective energy, but we must import most of our minerals, which produce our alloys. We may be able to import many of them from Mexico and the Dakotas, but if we are cut off from them, it is going to put us in a real pinch to produce the metal and composite products we have been supplying to our vital industries.

"We have been building a surplus over the last two years to take advantage of the prices, but even at that, we only have a six-month supply. We could increase our purchasing while we wait to find out if the UN is going to act and what they may do. Overall, I believe we will be able to supply steel and basic metals to the auto industry, but for the aircraft industry, we have limited resources of the trace minerals we need."

Steven looked grimly over to Jake Dustin for an overview. "Well, Jake, do you want to finish up this little shindig?"

Jake has been with Steven since they were both young wildcatters and considered themselves brothers. He has been through thick and thin in the oil business, but he always had a knack for finding the wells that hit. Even though he has a gambling streak in the business, he was the one who kept the numbers in line and was the level-headed one. When Steven proposed something like the biggest risk they had ever undertaken to see if his theory of draining the reserve would work, Jake provided the logistics and costs associated with such a giant undertaking, as well as the potential gain. He was able to show the potential trillions they could make if they could purchase all the dry wells and turn them into gushers. After they found Steven's idea worked, it was how they could quietly purchase those wells without being discovered, which is what Jake mastered in.

"Steven, we have been looking into this for a few years now since they have threatened us before. The issue we have this time around is we may not have the United States allying with us to stop the UN. They have gotten themselves in such horrible shape financially; they need the tax revenues we could provide worse than the UN. President Stewart is going to speak in front of the General Assembly and has asked Steven to also speak there and give our case as to why we cannot afford and refuse to pay their excessive taxes, which could be from fifteen to fifty percent, depending on how they want to classify us.

"We really won't have any idea what they will be doing until they have their assembly, but if it's anything like they did to China and Iraq, we are likely going to see the upper end as well as severe regulatory laws. They may reduce our production and development, and who knows what else they are capable of! This is going to be a tough fight, but one thing about Texans, we know how to fight."

"Thanks, Jake, and yes, we will fight this to our last breath. Y'all know how I feel about the UN and whether they will have our best interests at heart. They see what we have accomplished and believe they had a hand in it, so they feel they should be paid for their worldwide services. If that worked, how come there are more poor countries now than when they started? If they really wanted to stop poverty, they would copy our model, but they do not want to or are afraid to take their hands off the wheel and let their citizens make their own decisions. Therefore, we have been successful since we allow individuals to succeed or fail on their own merit and start over until they do succeed without government interference.

"So, gentlemen, we need to prepare for the worst and purchase as much raw material inventory as we can to prepare for this war. We do not know if it will be a political, economic, or shooting war, but we need to prepare ourselves for a long siege to hold out if we can. We are the foundation of the Texas economy, so we need to make sure that foundation is as strong as we can make it. You all need to fill your warehouses and get on your knees every day because very soon, we may be back in the Alamo. Dismissed."

As they were logging off their headsets, Steven looked over at Dave Scott. "Dave, you want to get a bite with Drake and me before we head down to Houston for the flight to Beijing?"

"Sure, Steve, give me a couple of minutes to make a couple of calls from my office. I don't usually like to eat anything before liftoff, and there is a great restaurant at the sky port in Beijing, so I may just have a quick snack."

"All right, how about we meet at my hanger in forty-five minutes, and we will take the corporate hover limo down to Houston Space and give us a few minutes to prepare for the Chinese delegation. They may be a key to this entire problem, and if we can get their support, it could be to our advantage. The Chinese coalition has some strong allies in the United Nations."

June Darling could not get Steven Moses off her mind. Was he really flirting with her, and what could he see in her that he does not see in the models and starlets she sees him around on the news programs from morning to night? He was easily the most eligible bachelor in Texas who is not only perhaps the richest man in the world but was a handsome guy. His long legs and wide shoulders made him the kind of real man every woman would want, and then the handsome, rugged features from working on the rigs give him confidence in himself that very few men have anymore. Of course, those deep gray-green eyes and thick blondish hair don't hurt… what is she thinking? Why would he be interested in a journalism professor in Austin? *Get a hold of yourself, June Darling.*

He did ask her out or at least made it obvious he wanted to see her again to do the interview. Perhaps she would do the interview just to see if she were imagining things or—

She was interrupted by a knock on her door. "June, are you in?"

"Yes, come in, Sally."

It was Sally Sherwood, Dean of the Journalism School and her closest friend.

"Hi, June. I have a favor to ask you that means a lot to the university and our journalism school."

"What is it, and why are you asking me?"

"Well, you've obviously been following the United Nations' attempted takeover of Texas, and we have been contacted by a large donor who wants us to cover it and document it for historical purposes. Since you authored your thesis on Steven Moses during the secession, the board has decided you would be the best person to document this and make a historical record about this event. We don't know what and where it's going, but we believe it may be one of the biggest historical events in Texas' short history and perhaps the United Nations. Our donor wants to make sure that our side of the issue is discussed and reported, and we think you are the perfect person to handle this research.

"We will be giving you a sabbatical from your teaching, and any expenses you will have will be paid by the university. I don't think I have to tell you, June, this is a once-in-a-lifetime opportunity for a journalist. It could lead to a book, and who knows what else."

"Well, thank you, Sally. I don't know what to say. You've caught me off guard, and, yes, it is interesting for me to record the historical details of these events as they happen; but I'm in the middle of the semester, and my students need me."

"June, we have contacted Professor Albertson to take your place, and your students will understand. They are journalists and know the magnitude of this opportunity as well as the historical significance. This is freedom and open markets against tyranny and socialism fighting for the final death of capitalism worldwide. We need you to record this fight. Can we count on you, June?"

"I don't know; this is all so sudden, and I don't know if I can do this. It would take so much time, and I would obviously have to go to New York to report it, I don't know.... Yes, I do! Someone once told me, 'Never wait for the next taxi when the one you need to take is parked right in front of you.' This may be the biggest mistake of my life or the taxi I need, so, yes, yes, I will take your proposal...er...offer."

"Here's hoping this isn't the only proposal you get."

"Sally, Stop!" June shrieked as she turned a bright shade of red.

"Well, there are all sorts of rumors floating around about his visit during his speech. You never know, and he is available, rich, and handsome—other than that, not much of a catch. Some girls have all the luck!"

"Stop it, he was just being nice. I am sure he is that way with everybody, and that is not why I'm doing this. He is handsome, though."

"From what I've heard, he was being way more than just nice. It sounded like he was pretty interested in our little professor."

"Quit! Where did you hear that?"

"A little birdie told me; I have my sources. You know how faculty are: telegraph, telephone, or tell a professor!"

"Yes, I will cover this story, but there is no way he is interested in me."

"Something tells me you are interested in him. June Moses has a nice ring to it, don't you think?"

"With friends like you, who needs enemies? Let's go have coffee." She laughed as they walked out her door.

Terry Thomas focused his investigation on the area of the last sighting of the intruder. There was no signal found on any of the sensors or radar. No one could understand how any farmers or even the better military craft could deflect all the technology they had on the border. It must have been a military aircraft with advanced software, which meant it had to be a US craft invading Texas, meaning an act of war if caught. Why would America take a risk like that just to look at some jackrabbits and to look around North Texas? If they try it again, he will be ready and will get a shot off.

He practiced his evasive maneuvers. Even with the limitations of this hover jet, he was able to push its capabilities. The new weapons were more responsive and had a nice feel with the visual responders and the intuitive spotters.

The techs back at the base upgraded his detection software and gave him a bit more distance and power on his weaponized lasers if he ever had a chance to take a shot. It felt like his mech-techs had tweaked his engines and handling a bit. His hover jet felt like it had more power and speed than it had before. Pretty standard when an event like the possible intruder happens. There were reasons to believe someone may be testing the response and detection technology.

He also could see the techs have been working on the wall and border zones, checking the detection lasers, as well as making sure everything was working as it should. He slowed as he approached the area to see if he noticed anything out of the ordinary to explain how they could get through the illuminated wall of detection. He was not interested in the jackrabbits scurrying across the field, trying to avoid becoming dinner for the local predators. He was more interested in the winged predators who were hunting for another type of dinner.

He pulled on the throttle, so he was hovering at one hundred feet and looked north toward the direction he thought the intruder had come from. Where up there could they be coming from? There were no bases for a couple of hundred miles, and breaking Texan airspace just doesn't seem worth the risk of being shot down. Suddenly, his alarms lit his windshield while pushing his craft into evasive maneuvers. "Laser lock, laser lock—take evasive action. Enemy aircraft targeting."

He automatically pushed toward the deck to get as low as he could while scanning the horizon with his lasers, finding nothing. He hid behind a tree, although if somebody shot, he would have bit it. Then, just as suddenly, a shock wave hit him. Something just roared past him, doing at least Mach 3, heading north again, and was gone before he could get his targeting software aimed. He fired one distant shot in the general spread direction he thought it might be heading.

"Hit, hit, hit." He got a hit around hundred-fifty miles out, and suddenly his Lasdar lit up with an aircraft heading northwest at Mach 3.5 and left his range at three hundred miles. What was it, and where was it going were the first questions, but what was an aircraft doing here in Texas that would take a chance like that and not be detected? How has it been able to get into the country without us seeing it? He'd better get back to the base and see if there was any information on his computer to help identify the bogey.

He took one last look around and banked back to the base as his windshield lit up again!

"Laser lock, laser lock, laser hit." As his cockpit erupted in flames, it crashed into the brush before he had a chance to pull the ejector.

A second jet blasted invisibly past as he faded into darkness. He laid in the wreckage and thought at least he died a free man doing what he loved as everything faded to black.

Arriving in Beijing was always a shock for the body, no matter how many times Steven had done it. Walking into that shuttle with the other twenty people getting ready to get strapped into a hundred-ton ramjet and shuttle glider is a nerve-racking experience. Even though everything was perfectly safe, to know that you are attached to something that travels eight thousand miles an hour gets your heart racing. When you hear the countdown start and the engines begin to rumble, suddenly you are being smashed into your seat by three Gs, turning you into a human pizza. Once the conventional rockets stop and the ramjet booster ignites, you either blackout or nearly do for the five-minute burn. Your breathing gets forced, and you must rely on your G-suit and ventilator mask to keep the circulation into your brain. The exhilaration of accelerating to those speeds, however, is a pure adrenaline rush.

In a matter of minutes from liftoff, you turn weightless as you leave the earth's atmosphere where you are surrounded by pure darkness yet the brightest sun you will ever see. In space is where you can really accelerate up to max speed before you begin reentry, and the shuttle turns into a ball of fire, dropping out of the sky until you begin lining up for the landing onto the Beijing National runway. If you enjoy adrenaline the way Steven did, there was no more thrilling ride available, and thanks to their secretly refined propellants and ramjet technology, Lone Star Air was the only provider to have a service to those whose time was measured by millions of dollars per hour.

Sure, it was only a two-hour flight, but blasting off and reentry were always tough on the body. Taking those kinds of Gs, even if it were a public craft, took a lot out of you and especially since they would be pulling the same Gs on the way back in another twelve hours. They all knew they needed to get Premier Zuan on their side, or they were going to have a hard time with the assembly.

They were escorted into the main boardroom, where Premier Zuan was seated with his Vice Premier Chua and the Minister of Energy Baoto, as well as the Oil, Coal, and Gas Secretaries. The hall was completely covered in rich dark mahogany with pictures of their accomplishments as an economic superpower. The Workers Party posters had long been torn down and replaced with pictures of skyscrapers and giant dams and factories. The Mao jackets had been replaced with some of the finest silk suits designed by the best tailors in the world. The fit and hand-tailoring were benefits from having nearly free skilled labor. Premier Zuan came around from the table to greet his guests as their hospitality was still an important part of their business culture.

"Welcome, Mr. Moses, Mr. Drake, and Mr. Scott. Thank you for coming; we are honored. I hope your flight went well. Sometimes you will have to let me fly in your shuttle. Such a great advancement since it takes us twelve hours to fly to Texas, and that is with a tailwind. Please have a seat. Can we get you something to eat? You must be hungry, and we cooked a special meal for our friends. We had our chefs make some lobsters and Chinese dishes you should enjoy."

The Republic of Texas

Steven smiled and responded, "Thank you so much, Premier Zuan. We are honored to be here, and we have become good friends over the few years we have known you and your cabinet. We value our relationship and are determined to continue to have you as one of our largest consumers of our petroleum products. We understand your dependence on us and our dependence on you as a supplier of commercial products to Texas."

After a most delicious meal, Steven got right to the point.

"Premier Zuan, Vice Premier Chua, Minister Baoto, and Secretaries, as you are aware, the United Nations is continuing talks to begin forcing us to pay to their world fund as well as become regulated by their energy commissions. If this were to happen, we would see our production costs go up dramatically as well as being regulated into not being able to produce our resources as efficiently as we can today. This would curtail our production and not allow us to be as reliable as we are now. These and other issues are our concerns for our business relationship, and we are hoping you will help stop this from happening with your veto vote on the Security Council.

"Cost-effective and reliable energy is a primary need for the world economies. If they were to force us to raise prices or curtail production, it would not only hurt us but you and every other world customer. Your country and people have benefited as much as any from a reliable supply of low-priced oil products. We are hoping you will help us put pressure on the United Nations not to impose these restrictions on Texas and our production."

Premier Zuan looked at Steven and smiled. "Mr. Moses, Mr. Drake, and gentlemen, we have been very satisfied with our relationship. We provide the world with our goods, and to produce those items, we not only need a cost-effective labor charge but unlimited and low-priced dependable energy. We have lots of electrical energy with our coal plants, which are very powerful and clean, and we have many available mines in our country; but we do not have oil and gas in the amounts we need and those you supply. We are pleased with our services from Moses Oil as you have been able to produce at prices below the rest of the world producers. This has been a good relationship between our two countries.

"Unfortunately, we are strong members in the United Nations and agree with most of what they are doing for the world. We have seen too much starvation and poverty around the world, which leads to riots and wars. There is much work that could be done if we were all pulling the cart together rather than separately to pull those poor countries out of their misery and help them to become more self-sufficient. If the Republic of Texas were to help pull this cart, there are no limits to the potential the world would have.

"My economic minister has also informed me that another one of our aluminum companies is relocating to the Republic of Texas. It was one of our stronger companies employing over a thousand workers. We have some immensely powerful coal plants that have a low cost to produce electricity, but they cannot compete with your NatGas plants since you basically get it for free as a byproduct of producing oil and from your abundant fracked gas resources. This is concerning to us that you can take our businesses from us simply because you produce gas cheaper than we can produce coal.

"At this point, we cannot sign a long-term agreement for our oil needs into the future. We will honor our agreements for the remainder of this quarter but will wait for the decision of the United Nations on how we want to do business in the future. We are receiving offers from other oil producers and will be comparing with them what they will be available to provide from their schedules and pricing. We are not saying we will not be using your energy in the future, but we would highly advise you to cancel your contract with the aluminum company as well as to become a member of the UN. Until both of those issues are resolved, we really have nothing to discuss."

Steven waited to let the words sink in before he spoke. "Premier Zuan, I certainly understand your concerns about the competition we are to you and the rest of the world. I also understand your loyalty to the United Nations, as you have been a member since its formation. What I do not understand is why you would expect us to damage our own country and markets to satisfy some world government, which, as you know, is filled with corruption and back-scratching deals. We have been against their overreach since we declared our independence, and we see nothing that has changed or altered our opinion.

"Premier Zuan and ministers, we believe every country and industry needs to be able to compete on an equal field where the best and most efficient producers will win the day. We believe the only way you can do that is through the free market and an openly capitalistic form of government. In that environment, the human spirit can grow and develop to innovate and create in a healthy competition to produce the best product possible. As these products and people's ideas compete against each other, the technology and products get better and better, forcing products to reach their full potential in both quality and cost.

"Premier, you need to grant your people and designers the freedom to grow their capabilities for their betterment. Your people have been enslaved to a top-down mentality rather than bottom-up creativity. You need to show the courage to allow your people the freedom to become more entrepreneurial rather than being nothing more than living, breathing machines. I know that may be an exaggeration, but you get the point of what I am saying. Why don't you take your first space shuttle ride with us tonight? There are a couple of extra seats, and you can visit Texas and see how freedom and a totally free market works and how it could work in your country."

"You don't understand our country or our people, Mr. Moses. We were centuries old when you were just settling in Texas, and our people are a proud and determined culture. We need a strong governance structure to bring diverse cultures together. We have been a one-party government for nearly a century, which has cleaned our country of corruption and has helped make us more efficient than we were even five years ago."

"With all due respect, Premier Zuan, you still have so much top-down interference that your industries have a tough time competing in the free market unless you force your workers to produce below their worth. For instance, you were talking about your coal energy plants producing the lowest-cost energy of any industrial country, but you mark up the cost to your own industries a thousand percent to bring revenue into your government. If you were staying competitive in the market, you would mark it up no more than double or triple and still generate good revenues allowing your industries to become profitable.

"Rather than stifling your businesses and people to generate revenues for Beijing, allow them to grow and expand the economy for everybody, including the government. That is what takes courage. Why don't you clear your schedule and come see capitalism and the free market at work and take your first trip outside the atmosphere to personally experience the very best way to travel ever developed?"

"That is a very tempting offer, Mr. Moses, and I see how you became the man you are. Okay, I will take my first ride in your space shuttle. Let me make the arrangements and call my wife. I will meet you at Lone Star Air in two hours."

"Thank you, Premier Zuan. We will have you back here tomorrow evening, and you will have had the ride of your life, even if it is for only a couple of hours. If Mrs. Zuan would like to come, bring her along, and we will show her some Texas hospitality. Has she had real Texas barbecue?"

THE STORM BUILDS

Secretary-General Polentas never liked waiting for anybody, even when it was for a United States president. The flight down from New York was uneventful for her and her counsel other than the usual disturbances you see once you hover outside of the compound. She could see the gangs rampaging the neighborhoods and raining violence on the people who could not afford to move away. It did seem there were more people hanging from the lampposts than normal. They had their usual handmade execution signs attached to them; there were two bankers, a stockbroker, an oil trader, and a pastor with what looked like his family all hanging with their arms extended. They were all guilty of various crimes against their community. The odd thing she had never seen was three were hanged on one lamppost, and they all had "Gangster" attached to their chests and NYTR under the word. Was there some sort of battle starting between the rival gangs?

Flying into Washington, DC, was more of the same, only the police had it pushed out a bit farther than New York had. When will these Americans ever understand that we all need to work together to make this work for everyone?

President Chambers' secretary Ann Fletcher entered the room. She was an attractive middle-aged woman with brownish blonde shoulder-length hair woven into a tight French weave. She looked like she might be of Irish descent, obviously well put together with her tan business suit and knee-length skirt, highlighting her attractive figure. "President Chambers and the congressional leaders are ready to see you. Is there anything you would like, Secretary-General Polentas?"

"No, thank you, Ms. Fletcher, please, just show me the way."

Secretary Fletcher led her to a West Wing conference room appointed with a long table, which had the president at the head with his cabinet and congressional leaders on the right side. The atmosphere was tense as everybody knew the Secretary-General was there to make sure there was cooperation with their upcoming talks on the Texas resolution.

President Chambers rose and came around the table to greet her. "Hello, Secretary-General, welcome to the White House. I hope you didn't have a long wait. We were having some extensive discussions and hope you will understand. Have a seat at the head of the table, and let's get right to business."

"Thank you, President Chambers, Vice President, cabinet members, and congressional leaders. We are so glad to be here. Washington, DC, is so beautiful this time of year. I understand why you are proud of your historic city. I used to visit this city when I was a child with my father when he was an ambassador and just loved all the monuments and parks that make this city so special.

"As you all know, we are working on a resolution that will ensure the Republic of Texas finally become a full member of the United Nations. There is no reason for them to continue to use and exploit all the infrastructure and protection the United Nations provides and not have to share in the payment for those benefits. They have the free and safe passage of their products to and from ports of origin to their port facilities and pay no duties or fees for those services. They trade on our markets and use our banking arrangements as well as all our international armies and currencies and pay nothing to our United Nations funds. We have allowed it, since, for a certain time from their secession, we agreed with you that they needed time to establish their industries, but now they are the most prosperous nation in the world and in large part, thanks to our infrastructure, we have provided for their marketplace.

"Everybody knows they have contributed nothing to the International Military Fund or contributed troops for our peacekeeping missions around the world, giving them the stability to conduct their business. This gives them a distinct advantage in their markets by not having to pay the investments the rest of the world is paying to keep up the infrastructure, aid programs, and peacekeeping forces, which is unfair to the world. If we and you must purchase their products, then they should contribute to the world we have made for them to operate, which is why UN Resolution 2033–311 has been proposed."

President Chambers adjusted his seat forward and interrupted, "Madam Secretary, everyone here agrees with everything you have said and supports the concepts you are proposing. Texas has enjoyed a free ride on the backs of the rest of the world with its unregulated exploitation of the earth and all its precious minerals and energy products. We, too, believe it is time for Texas to contribute their fair share to maintain all the world government infrastructure and security they use to produce and promote their economy. We think there are going to be some issues they may resist since they are so stuck in their ways of free enterprise and capitalism without government intrusion. Do you plan to enforce the UN World Environmental Agency regulations on them, and will you have UN officials there to verify that enforcement?"

"Well, of course, President Chambers. The World Environmental Agency is all that is protecting our water to make sure it is healthy to drink and our air is clean to breathe. The agency has evidence they have been using unapproved technology for their industries and are polluting well beyond the levels we have mandated as safe. So, of course, we would need to monitor their emissions like every other UN member to maintain and validate those emissions. It is simply to not only protect the earth's air and water but to level the playing field for the other nations. We are proud to say that last year was the most pollution-free per capita throughout the world, thanks in large part to the World Environmental Agency and their enforcement agencies."

Vice President Victoria Price spoke up, "Madam Secretary, we certainly understand the need for the WEA and the wonderful accomplishments they have made around the world to help save our precious environment. You also must understand the precarious position we are in being a former country with them as well as our necessity to use and maintain their power generation. Energy Secretary Phillips has made a detailed study over the past year and has found we are purchasing forty-five percent of our energy from Texas, and if they were to cut us off, we would have an immediate power blackout as our power substations would fall like dominoes across the country. We have an antiquated transmission system that loses over ten percent of what we produce or buy in the transmission of our energy through the grid. Obviously, New York would also be affected, so do you have any suggestions on how we can replace their production?"

"I understand your concerns, Vice President Price, and we have some of the same concerns having our headquarters in New York, so we have made some concessions into the agreement. We have contracted both Canada and Mexico to use them as alternative providers. They have agreed to call for emergency rationing of their countries to supply you an additional ten percent each. We can also pass an emergency war waiver to lift the mothballed coal-fired plants on a temporary basis until the potential crisis is over. This should give you enough energy to maintain your own emergency rationing to help stabilize the grid to keep the basic services and governments as well as the strategic industries operating for at least six months. We do have some concerns about more unrest as there would be more shortages, but the added revenues would bring more prosperity to the world."

"Excuse me, Secretary Polentas," Vice President Price responded. "It will take months to acquire the necessary coal and to recommission one of those aging plants. We closed those coal mines years ago, and bringing it from the Chinese miners in the West would cost too much. We need a more immediate solution, or we could have massive blackouts."

President Chambers replied, "We have our concerns about the security and peace of our country. As you know, we already are having security and gang problems inside our cities with multiple lynchings and violence and really don't know how much more chaos we can withstand. Six months is a long period of time for us to watch this continue to collapse before we can expect any recovery. We would obviously prefer to not have to go through this and would like you to convince Texas to agree without any military action. If you take military action, we will want it to be a very short event so we can begin to recover. Have you addressed the economic and labor issues they would need to accept to become a member of the UN?"

"We will have to address their lack of labor representation in their workforce. They will have to have to accept fair and equal labor laws as well as maintain a Department of Labor Fairness to make sure they have a fair and equitable living wage and all the benefits that go along with those laws. They also will have to report to the UN Economic Fairness Panel to share their technologies as well as equalize their contracts with our member countries. By our estimation, they are completely out of balance with the UN economic rules and regulations."

Senate Leader Dalton Young spoke up, "As you know, Madam Secretary, they are also out of compliance with the UN hate speech resolutions by maintaining numerous churches, which discriminate against homosexuality and women's rights as well as other intolerant dialogue and would like to know how you would address those issues?"

"Of course, Senator Young, and congratulations on your daughter's election. We would require them to agree that their church leaders take a more tolerant stance to their extremist rhetoric like they do in the US and other countries. Unfortunately, some of those pastors have had to be jailed or relieved of their duties for their insistence to defy our resolutions. We have made some progress since the Bible ban and may have to institute that, of course, to maintain the peace. They will find in short order these adjustments will make for a more civil and respectful dialogue both inside and outside their churches. We still have some resistance, but for the most part, the churches have learned to moderate their messages to become more tolerant of other people's freedom of lifestyle.

"We would like to invite President Chambers to speak in front of the UN General Assembly in preparation for the writing and issuance of the Texas Acceptance Resolution 2033-311 two weeks from this Friday and have invited President Stewart and his delegation to also speak before the assembly. Nobody is going to say we didn't give them every opportunity to make their case."

June Darling opened her e-mail to chat with her father when she saw a high-priority mark. It read:

"June Bug, I received this e-mail from someone I don't know and thought you might be interested in seeing it."

The message read:

Pastor Darling,

I call myself the Texas Ranger, and I need some help advancing the name of Jesus. I have scrambled my destination, so you can't get in touch with me, and more importantly, neither can the United Nations. I belong to a group called the Texas Christ Church of New York, and we are taking back our church and America. We sell Bibles in the underground economy and need more than we have available. We are importing them and have a large and growing network of Christians wanting their Bibles back, and we are able to smuggle them to the closed churches.

We have also formed a peacekeeping group that is taking back New York City, one neighborhood at a time. We have caught, tried, and convicted several gangsters who have been punished accordingly. We need somebody to help us acquire Bibles, but just as important, we need someone to get our message out to America and the world without risking their own lives. We know your daughter is a very well-respected journalist in Texas and would like to have her publish

*our story and let people know we are out here. Can
you help us? I will call tomorrow night at eight your
time. If you can help me, please answer so we can
talk.*

June returns:

*Daddy, please have him contact me; it may add to my
new research project.*

Love, June Bug

The flight back was uneventful for Steven, but Premier Zuan had the
ride of his life. He was sweating like a convicted man walking to the
gallows on takeoff, but when he went weightless, he began playing like
a five-year-old boy. He wanted to know everything there was about the
flight and how fast they were crossing time zones around the world. He
had everybody spin him and float from one end of the shuttle and back.
He had them spin him in somersaults till he got a bit dizzy before the
descent started. He even got strapped in with the pilots on the landing
while seeming to have a smile chiseled into his face. He apologized that
his wife Laoa would not come since she said she was too afraid to ride the
shuttle and tried to talk him out of it, but nobody could do that.

On landing, he came over to Steven and shook his hand while bow-
ing. "Thank you, Mr. Moses, that was a thrill of a lifetime. It was everything you said it was and more—what a flight! I felt like I weighed a ton
on the liftoff, and the speed the shuttle could travel was so surprising!
Then within minutes, you are weightless. To see the world from space
and look out into space with all the stars and moon was something I will
never forget. Then to finish it off, you re-enter in a ball of fire as you fall
like a rock from over a hundred miles up, leaving your stomach in space

was terrifying yet exhilarating. I almost vomited on the way down, but the thrill was more than I ever imagined. What a ride! Mr. Moses, you have an unbelievable aircraft!"

"Call me, Steven, Premier," he said as he handed him an '18,000 MPH Club' shirt. "Yes, it is quite a bit of technology, but it serves a valuable purpose as a time saver for us. We needed to be able to travel back and forth to your capital on a regular basis, which would normally take three days minimum and a recovery time of another two days. That is a full week for people who are making multibillion-dollar transactions day in and day out.

We realized a long time ago we could not afford taking those people out of circulation for those lengths of time, so one of the first things we did when we became a country was to develop faster and faster methods of flight until we were able to travel anywhere in the world in three hours. Once we were able to combine the technological advancements with fuel development, we had a commercial rocket shuttle that was ready for public use. This made business sense as well as a flight like no other. That is what capitalism and ingenuity do for the economy and society. Let's take the corporate hover limo, and I will give you the tour of our company and south Texas."

They took the short walk over to the Moses hangars, where the eight-man limousine and pilot were waiting to take them on the tour of Moses Industries. It was a sleek craft, which was simply a luxury limousine built to fly at over three hundred knots from site to site while talking with your guests. It had good speed and power yet was quiet as an empty church inside. The pilot loaded the premier's luggage into the trunk and gave him the copilot seat, which had the best view of the ground while speaking to him on the headphones. Once the passengers were on board, he started the hover jets, lifting them to height before the turbo thrusters fired and headed them toward the port facilities.

Steven looked out as the south Houston coast came into view, and the oil port covered the horizon. "Premier, this is our main port where we receive the inbound oil tankers as well as your outbound gas and oil mixtures that come from and go to every country in the world. These tankers will go through our expanded Panama Canal, which we have widened and expanded into two-way traffic for more efficiency. There are normally around one hundred tankers coming or leaving this area at any given time with no accidents over the past twenty years. Tankers can arrive and load or unload at one of these in port or offshore terminals in less than three hours.

"As we travel inland, you can see our refineries, which are the largest and most efficient anywhere in the world. Our oil cracking separators are producing at rates double the world average, each one cracking tankers worth of oil every fifty minutes. This process produces enormous volumes of natural gas, enough to supply the world's needs every day, which we have converted into the electrical generation you were asking me about in our meeting. Yes, we have very low costs for our electricity as a byproduct of our oil production.

"As you look down, you will see over five hundred NatGas electrical generation plants. We not only produce enough electricity for all of Texas but sell our excess to the United States. This is a large part of why we paid back our loan before it was due. We are continually investing in more plants and grid infrastructure to give us the lowest cost energy of any country around the world. We are close to having the ability to send electricity across the ocean floor through high-density submarine cables that could reach Europe with little bleed loss. We know you have the second-lowest-cost, but as we talked about in your meeting with your corruption and province costs, those low prices for coal power are lost. Imagine if you were able to expand your low-cost energy and send it to Japan, Korea, and the Middle East?

"Now, down below us is our high-energy usage manufacturers such as aluminum, steel, aircraft, computer, and strategic metals production. These companies are not a part of Moses Industries but are located here due to the low cost and short transmission of our power plants. They receive discounted energy rates during the off-peak hours or seasons, helping both their production costs and the energy companies using the surplus energy. These companies have found not only a low cost of energy, but our low tax rates give them a cost advantage very few countries can offer. They have fled from the high-tax countries like the United States or the European Union to set up shop here just as they do in China."

"I understand completely, Steven Moses. You are taking many of our companies which can lower costs the same way they have come to our country in the past. This, of course, is of concern to us since you have an advantage of not having to pay the United Nations funds that the rest of us pay."

"Premier, I understand your concerns. However, we would work much better as partners rather than competitors on these issues. We can help you build your economy in a freer market framework rather than the communist model you are following now. This will make you more competitive as you learn efficiencies in your industries. You know as well as I do that you are not getting what you are paying for with the United Nations taxes. We can help you take advantage of the natural, technological advancements the free and unfettered ingenuity that comes from the entrepreneurial spirit.

"Once you take the controls off the human spirit, they are free to try innovative ideas and explore the power of trial-and-error to develop new and advanced technologies that can compete in the marketplace. As you can see across the Texas horizon, there is business after business, all producing goods and services for both the local economy and the world. Every one of these started as somebody's idea or dream and is his way of reaching his dream without interference of an overregulating and frankly corrupt government. You will not see this anywhere else in the world, and just look how well it is working with your own eyes."

They flew over hundreds of miles of businesses, watching trucks running every direction as evidence of commerce being transacted by the invisible dance of capitalism. This dance has been going on for centuries; however, now it was playing to its own music, and the results spoke for themselves. The only thing that appeared constant was the activity and the growing miles of businesses on the edges of the horizon. The pilot banked the limo jet to the east as they headed to the Moses Skyscraper, where some Texas-sized brisket and baby back ribs were being prepared for their most honored guest.

Steven welcomed Premier General Zuan with a few words of tribute to the Chinese leader and finished with, "Premier Zuan, we hope you will become our partner in the new world we are building with our free-market model. It has brought prosperity to more countries and people than any other economic system. Tonight, though, we hope to show you how Texas is truly famous for two things, oil and barbecue, and as Chef Holt says, his baby backs will make you want to slap your grandma; they are so good! Welcome to Moses Tower, and enjoy your stay."

Premier Zuan looked confused by the translation but saw the crowd laughing; he joined along as he was handed a black cowboy hat and alligator boots with the state of Texas engraved on them to try on. After he was dressed up for real Texas barbecue, he was grinning from ear to ear.

"Hello, is this Professor Darling?"

"Yes. Who is this?"

"Hi, Professor Darling, I call myself the Texas Ranger, and your father, Pastor Darling, gave me your headset number. He said you would be expecting my call and gave your permission to talk to me and hear our story."

"Yes, I did, but why all the secrecy, and why is your number scrambled, showing a Brazilian identifier?"

"You don't understand, Professor. We are some of the most wanted people in the United States and especially in New York. We are considered enemies of America and the UN police for smuggling Bibles into the United States. We can be jailed for ten years for spreading hate. We are one of the fastest-growing underground organizations with some of the most talented people in New York, so we can communicate very well to the outside by scrambling our locations. We are a closed group and are continually on the move, so it is very hard for the government police to find or capture us. This is also a safety measure for you as my voice is altered, as is the background noise to throw off the authorities who would otherwise be able to locate this in less than four minutes."

"Sounds very James Bond, but I suppose I understand since you are technically breaking the law by smuggling Bibles and running an underground church. Why did you choose me to tell your story?"

"One of the main reasons is, you are from Texas where you still have freedom of the press. If I were to tell my story to a journalist here, they would be required to report us to the police if they were not already working for the government to help find churches. We have read your stories, and we see you give free-market economics and businesses a fair voice, so we wanted to give you our story and thought you would report it accurately.

"We have been a movement for nearly three years and are the largest organized church in New York. We are selling over two million Bibles a year in the underground economy as well as all types of outlawed or restricted items. This has given us a strong monetary position that has helped us in our latest movement while fighting the gangs and sweeping the streets of these murderers. We have set up a neighborhood police force that is taking back the streets one block at a time.

"You have to understand what it is like to live in New York nowadays. The city has become a human jungle where survival is New Yorkers' single thought from minute to minute. The gangs control the neighborhoods, and they are always fighting over territory and control of the black markets.

"Anybody who can't afford to get out of the city or is not a member of a gang is going to be a victim of the gangs to be robbed, raped, or killed. They have targeted capitalists such as bankers or stockbrokers as criminals, and they're lynched as a warning to others. They consider making money a crime against the community. There are no safe places left in New York anymore, and especially at night, it becomes a survival zone.

"There are a number of gangs, and the police are all owned by them, so they have free reign to terrorize the people. They control the streets through violence and intimidation as well as by demanding protection money from all the businesses, which is then paid to the unions. The strongest gang is the Dockworkers, who control all the gangs through a complex network. We are not exactly sure where they get their funding and weapons, but they have a connection with the government. We are trying to figure out their connections, although we suspect they are directly or indirectly controlled by the UN.

"They use their intimidation tactics to threaten and kill anybody who stands in their way or attempts to stand up to them. They are also in control of banking and finance, and if anyone crosses them, they will soon end up hanging from a lamppost. Then one of the gang's people will be taking over their position, which keeps them in a constant state of terror, willing to do whatever the gangs demand.

"Many of the rebel gangs are simply anarchists who will go in and murder families for whatever reason they consider a hanging offense. The bankers and finance people, as well as Christians, have been so vilified, they are often killed for little or no apparent reason. The gangs use all types of violence and declare an open season on anybody who crosses them. The common citizens are simply available for their convenience to rob, beat, or rape for whatever reason they deem an offense.

"If a girl is raped on the street and reports a protected gang to the police, her family will be lynched within days. You do not cross the gangs, and especially the Dockworkers. This is who we have been targeting for our own retribution. We have our own courts with witnesses and defense, but if we capture them, it is for a legitimate reason.

"We have started a Christian group called the Texas Christ Church, which is beginning to fight the gangs and bring justice to the neighborhoods. We are growing quickly as the victims are looking for safety in numbers. In addition, a small revival is moving across the city from people looking for something to hold onto in Jesus Christ. Our members are all wanted criminals by the gangs since we have fought them in numerous neighborhoods and have tried and punished many in their own manner.

"We have been smuggling Bibles into the city, which has the police and authorities trying to stop it and put us in jail. Those of us who have been jailed are usually turned over to the gangs and hanged, with the others being shipped to prison camps around the country. It is a dangerous job and larger than we can succeed in doing, but we believe we are making a difference. We have some Texas Christ Church neighborhoods where the gangs have been thrown out and have agreed to leave them be, so there are some victories we are seeing block by block.

"We are hoping you will tell our story and let the world know what is going on in New York. We don't know everything but are finding out more and more every day as our movement grows. We have our suspicions of what the structure of these gangs is, but nothing is confirmed. We are hoping you will report it as we find things out and will be our voice to the outside world."

"Thanks, Ranger. I would be happy to send your story to syndication. Your timing is amazing since I just accepted a project that will mirror your story from another angle to expose what is happening in New York. There are winds blowing that are going to affect both New York and Texas, and I want to report the entire story, including yours. I look forward to talking to you in the future. Goodbye."

"Goodbye, Professor Darling."

TEXAS RESPONDS

Terry was leading a group of four hover jets along the border, looking for any signs of crossings by the aircraft that shot him down. He was laid up in the hospital for four weeks recovering from his injuries. Fortunately, the crash beacon went off, and thanks to the quick action of the medic craft, he was able to get to the emergency room in time to save his life. Texas has the best hospitals and doctors on the planet, and his recovery from his injuries was simply more evidence to him. They wanted to keep him longer, but they did not have enough rope to keep him tied down. He wanted to find out who or what was crossing this border.

Texas not only has the best medical system in the world but has some of the most creative medical insurance money can buy. Most Texans have policies like Terry, which are employer-assisted pay plans with higher deductibles and a cafeteria-style benefit program. You can have as many benefits covered or as few as you choose, but all of them take care of major medical for catastrophic events. His deductible is partially paid by his employer, and the remainder is paid in a twelve-month payroll deduction plan. This makes sure the doctors and hospitals are paid as well as making it painless for the patient. After twelve months, everybody is paid, allowing protection for the providers of the health care industry. There is intense competition for the doctors, as the best and brightest are continually competing for the more lucrative fields to keep their skills sharpened.

In America, he would have been in a hospital ward for months; however, with the technology and techniques these Texas hospitals have, he was out in only weeks. They wanted him to go a week or two longer, but he was going to get out as soon as he could and was not going to let some overprotective surgeon tell him no!

He really didn't remember much about the crash other than he was flying in the same area as he was before and suddenly was hit by a rogue aircraft that had entered Texan airspace. Why would they be invading Texas? What were they up to, and who was it?

"Rattler to wing, be prepared for a slow hover as we are approaching where I was hit and crashed."

"Roger that, flight leader. Bronco here. Do you want us to fly a perimeter as protection or stay close?"

"Roger that, Bronco, scatter and fly a ten-mile perimeter, and Chance will stay on my wing. You both know there have been a few other sightings here, so stay on your toes and monitor 100 miles out."

Terry fluttered to a stationary hover to take a good close look at what remained of his craft. The company had taken most of his hover jet back to the shop for forensics, but it was clear where he had crashed by the blackened brush and ground. He tried to look in the direction from where he felt he had been fired on and where the invader had come and fled. Nothing was coming to his mind as he cruised over to the north wall to see exactly where the sensors would have been located, trying to find how they were defeated. Even the latest stealth technology should not have allowed jets to cross undetected, but they did.

Suddenly, his display lit up from an aircraft coming over at Mach 2 from the north at three hundred miles and closing. As he tried to focus on a visual, it suddenly dropped off the screen and disappeared. Scanning the horizon, he saw nothing, although there was a contrail being formed by what must have been the jet when it suddenly turned vertical and twisted back north. He strained to see the shape and any markings, but even with his face mask magnification, there was no way to make out exactly what type it was. Perhaps a Mirage 2020, but it was impossible to tell. At least he did get an initial track before it disappeared, and the techs can get an engine match off it, although the chances of that were between slim and none.

The Republic of Texas

The Republic of Texas assembly was loud and filled with congressmen and senators from around the country. Each county had one senator and a congressman for each one hundred thousand citizens, and the country was set up exactly like the Founders of the United States with their three branches of government. This allowed for balance between the urban and rural areas of Texas, giving the republic equal representation. This assembly was the largest event since the secession. The President was going to discuss the upcoming fight against United Nations Resolution 2033–311and what it would mean to Texans. It was not only being broadcast across Texas but around the world. Even though the President was not a powerful office, he still was the figurehead of the Republic of Texas and would be the person who informed as well as representing the country in nationwide events. In this instance, because this resolution would have such powerful economic ramifications, he asked Steven to speak to the economics of the issue.

The Vice President walked in with Steven, who sat at the side with Drake and the presidential cabinet. Vice President Chavez approached the lectern. "Ladies and gentlemen, Texans, and people watching from around the world, this is not a time we have asked for and would prefer to not have an assembly like this. It is my great honor to introduce President Stewart of the Republic of Texas."

President Stewart entered from the side door in a tailored charcoal suit with black cowboy boots. He looked determined and stoic with his jaw set as he stood behind the podium, looking over the crowd. Then he began, "My fellow Texans, you have worked so hard to bring us to the point we are now. This has been the greatest experiment the world has ever seen, going from an energy-producing state in America to forming our own country and, within eight short years, rising to one of the most powerful economies in the world.

"As you know, the United Nations is in the process of writing a resolution that will handicap, if not destroy, this great economic engine, which literally powers the world. We have built this engine through the unleashed power of free-market capitalism, thereby freeing the human spirit to turn Texans' dreams into a reality. We have accomplished this since Texas believes it is better to have a healthy environment to grow their businesses than for the government to stand in their way with high taxes and stifling regulations. We believe in sensible taxes to encourage businesses to invest in people and regulations that strike a balance between protection and production. We believe businesses are respected citizens of Texas first and corporations second, so they maintain a healthy work environment as well as a healthy business environment. We trust these businesses to watch out for their people and to show the transparency to look out for their neighbors and neighborhoods.

"We trust in businesses to be honorable managers of their resources and environment, which has provided us with the cleanest, most efficient industries on earth. Our businesses are the safest anywhere, as their records will attest, which is one of the reasons we have the lowest regulatory costs and least amount of government interference, both working efficiently for all those involved. This has added to our overall efficiency, allowing these industries to have the highest compensation anywhere in the world without the conflict and cost of unions. These and numerous other free-market forces lower costs, allowing Texas to have some of the most cost-effective energy and manufacturing pricing of any producer in the world."

As Steven looked around the assembly, his eyes spotted someone in the balcony toward the back who he had not seen in quite a while. He noticed the wavy strawberry blonde hair immediately and could make out she was wearing a white suit and a yellow ribbon in her hair. He suddenly imagined the sweet lilac smell of the perfume she was wearing when he saw her at the university.

"We have been warned we will be expected to pay the standard thirty to thirty-five percent tax the rest of the new UN members pay. They say it is unfair for us to use the oceans and byways without having to pay for the protection they provide in the commerce lanes. We don't believe we should have to pay those fees and are willing to provide our own protection for those shipping lanes. We believe the shipping lane protection is only a small amount of the funds the UN takes in.

"Too much of their money is used to pay off corrupt governments and wasted for their own unethical activities, which have been documented numerous times. We do not believe in their Marxist ideals of income distribution from the wealthier countries to the poorer and are simply more of the same socialism we left when we separated from the United States. This is another government redistribution program that takes from the producers and gives to the nonproducing countries. We understand the only reason these poorer countries are struggling is due to corrupt communist governments stealing from their people. This is where they want to send our hard-earned profits—places we would rather see cleaned up.

"I could go on about this, but Steven Moses has prepared a report of what this potentially means to the Texan economy and our oil industry. So, to speak on the economic impact this would have on our republic, I would like to introduce Steven Moses."

A polite ovation spread across the chamber as Steven walked to the podium with his eyes and jaw set as he looked around the room.

"Ladies and gentlemen of Texas, you know who I am and the industries I represent. We are about to be asked to give up not only a significant percentage of our income here in Texas but also an equally large amount of our sovereignty. We have built the strongest economy in the world through hard work and innovative development, and technology. Our entire economy and country are built on the free flow of oil and our ability to produce it as cost-effectively as possible. These UN taxes will be adding as much as 35 percent to our costs, making our product less competitive to our businesses and industries. This not only punishes Texas but will also punish our customers around the world as well, including the United States, Japan, and China.

"Some will say this is only fair since the rest of the world must pay taxes to the United Nations. The rest of the nations chose to join the UN, and we have chosen not to join; and now we are being forced to join against our free will. We believe all countries should be free to join unions or not join such unions, and is a God-given right to individuals, countries, and industries. We see this UN Resolution as restrictive to our freedom and will hamper our sovereignty in numerous ways, both economically and socially.

"We have chosen to not have workers' unions for the same reason. We believe it stifles a person's ambition and creativity, so we allow workers to vote if they want unions. Repeatedly, our workers have freely voted against unions. The unions no longer try since they know our workers understand the shortcomings of forming unions and accepting mediocrity and watered-down achievement as well as income potential. This is one reason we have the highest productivity and wages of any country in the world.

"Just as on a small level, you have the same effect with a worldwide union, which stifles a country's ability to compete and achieve under the guise of fairness. Economically, it will affect the oil industry in both the cost and further development of our vital resources. In addition to adding the direct costs of taxes, we will also be subject to strict United Nations regulations over our industries, which will hamper our production and development.

"We have identified over ten thousand regulations that will interfere with the production and refining of oil and gas that will cause production to fall and costs to rise. These costs have been projected to increase costs anywhere from eighty to over one hundred percent of current expense. In addition, these regulations will interrupt much of our production and refinement, decreasing our output from twenty to thirty-five percent, depending on how the laws are interpreted.

"These costs will be passed on to our other industries, which depend on low-priced energy, causing their costs to increase, making their products less competitive on the world market. Many will be forced to move to countries that have lower expenses in other areas to compensate, such as labor or living expenses. This will be a major disruption to our industries and will drive up the costs worldwide for energy and production.

The increased prices of oil and gas will affect both costs and supplies on an already stretched commodity, which can potentially drive-up demand and prices exponentially to the end-users. This is going to be a burden to the entire world and affect the poor nations the worst. The poorer nations are exactly the ones who cannot afford these higher costs on their people, making them even more desperate. These costs will affect the very people who can afford them the least.

"In Texas, we believe in the freedom of the individual to pursue his dreams and desires without government interference. Whether that means raising a crop of wheat, drilling a well in hopes of hitting it rich, or casting a lure on a lake in hopes of catching a bass, we believe the individual has the right to decide what is best for him. We also believe the individual is the corporation, which is a collection of individuals pursuing their dreams and desires as an individual entity. The corporation should be free to chase their dreams without the interference of the government but should be allowed to decide what is best for it, just as the individual fishing for bass on the lake. Only they know what their own plans and dreams are in their own individual case.

"Finally, we are a Christian society that not only believes in God and Jesus Christ but that our churches have an absolute right to their freedom of worship. We cannot abide by the UN charter, which closes any church that preaches anything the UN finds offensive or considers hate speech. We will not allow our pastors and priests to be censored for what they believe, no matter how many people may deem their beliefs offensive. Jesus said that the world would find His words offensive and that the world would hate His words. Jesus said to love the sinner but hate the sin, while the world wants these churches to tolerate sin and, in many instances, to celebrate the sin. This goes completely contrary to Jesus' teaching, against our Constitution, and denies Texas its religious sovereignty. For these reasons and many more, we recommend this body and Texans to continue to stand against the membership into the United Nations. Thank you, and may God bless Texas."

As Steven turned to sit down, someone yelled, "Don't mess with Texas!"

A thunderous applause rolled across the chamber as every seat was emptied into a loud standing ovation and a chant of, "Don't mess with Texas!" Every corner of the building was standing and chanting as the defiance was made clear, not only in the building, but the message was also being sent across Texas and around the world that there was unity for freedom and sovereignty by the entire country. By this display, the vote was now a mere formality.

Steven looked across the assembly; his eyes went up into the balcony where he could see just the slightest hint of strawberry blondish hair where he knew Professor Darling was standing. It appeared that from what he could see, she, too, was standing and applauding, and for whatever reason, that was all that mattered to him at that moment. He knew because of her applause he had said what needed to be said.

He exited the stage before the politicians began the formal debate and votes for the passage of the Texan resolution to reject membership to the United Nations. It was more a formality as congressmen got airtime and let their constituents know they were standing up for them. He shook a few hands as he made his way to the door where he met Drake, asking him for a few minutes to go run a quick errand. Walking up the stairs to the balcony, he found the one person he was looking for as she sat trans-ponding notes of the debate.

He tapped her on the shoulder and watched her turn around in surprise and delight. He motioned her into the hallway where they could talk and reacquaint.

"I really liked your speech. It was brief and to the point, but you really spoke for all of us Texans. You not only covered the economics of the issue but the religious aspects of the takeover, which are just as important to our freedom."

The Republic of Texas

"Thank you, June, but that isn't why I came up here?"

"Oh, really, why did you?"

"Well, if you remember, you…ah…owe me a chance to take you to dinner, and I owe you an interview."

He enjoyed the way she turned into her pinkish shade of red as he stumbled on his words. "You mean now? You remembered our last conversation when I couldn't go? I must cover this event. I mean, I'm working on this project and—"

"You know as well as I that this is only a formality before they vote unanimously for the resolution. And besides, it's going to be recorded for later. You promised me the last time I could take you to dinner, and I know a special restaurant I think you will like—if you enjoy seafood."

"Where, what? I must go see Senator… oh, wait, what the heck! I *do* love seafood. When do you get a chance to have dinner with the wealthiest man in the world? Am I being too obvious?"

"No, not at all. Grab your things, and I will take you downstairs where I can rearrange my schedule with Drake to take the rest of the afternoon off."

"How did you know I was here? I didn't tell anybody I was coming. I just got my press pass and slipped up here in the balcony so I could record the event. Who told you I was here?"

"You were the only person I saw in the audience. Didn't you notice me staring at you?"

"No, I thought you were just looking at the audience. Let me grab my purse and things; then we can go."

She didn't know what to think about this: Steven Moses was treating her like more than the mousy professor she was. Why wasn't he going after all those models or high society women who were always around him on TV? Why did she have to wear this old suit she wore a hundred times, and her makeup was a mess in this humidity, let alone her hair? Why were her hands shaking? Maybe a quick trip to the ladies' room? Was she asleep, or was this real? She pinched her forearm while she gathered her things just to make sure. They took the elevator down to the dignitaries' lounge, where Jeff Drake was waiting. He seemed thrilled to see her and was happy to take them back to the office where Steven's private hover jet was waiting.

They changed hover jets, putting her things in the hatch and then helping her into his new Black Stallion. It was deep black with silver trim while having the streamlined shape of a sports hover that was built primarily for speed and looked like a flying Corvette. It was frightening yet thrilling all at the same time. She settled into the deep seat as the body bars lowered, locking her comfortably into place.

"Get ready for takeoff. This one has more speed than most and will be a little bouncy as we accelerate. I want to take you to one of my favorite spots in the Gulf."

"Are you sure you know how to fly thi—"

The Black Stallion was blasted off by two powerful jets with a stabilizer fan to allow for the hover while the two jets rotated horizontally, giving it thrust and power. She felt herself pushed straight back in the seat and could no longer feel the body bars on her chest from the force of the acceleration. She felt a sense of terror and thrill all at the same time. She hoped Steven was able to fly this as well as he seemed.

Once they reached cruising speed and altitude, she was treated to one of the most spectacular views of the Gulf she had ever seen. They were flying straight south over the water, and she could see the sun lowering toward the water reflecting the east, casting the skies into a blue-pink warmth, lighting the horizon into a pinkish-blue rainbow. They were flying at dizzying speeds, and Steven quickly proved he was an accomplished pilot, pointing out the different landmarks and oil derricks spread across the Gulf. He would drop down occasionally to point out a certain landmark as he gave her a tour of his workplace, and they talked about the day's events.

After an hour, they turned east, and she could see islands and derricks as well as ships coming and going while they screamed across the Gulf at speeds she had no idea existed in hover jets, even though this one made almost no noise. He played some nice gospel jazz on the sound system while she tried to take it all in.

"How fast are we going?"

"We are just a little over the sound barrier—about 760 miles per hour."

"Can you tell me where we're going yet?"

"It's a nice little restaurant in the Keys that has some of the best seafood in the Gulf."

"Oh my, a restaurant in the Florida Keys. I guess it was worth the wait since I only took you to the Longhorn Bistro, and you are taking me to the Keys! Do they allow peanut shells on the floor like the Longhorn? You're sure not very good at making trades."

He looked at her with a wink and laughed. "Oh, I don't know about that; seems a fair trade from my eyes," making her smile and blush.

She responded, "You really like embarrassing me, don't you?" making them both laugh.

She sat back and enjoyed the beautiful view of the Gulf as he flew in a meandering flight, pointing out more sights and islands as the sun sank lower into the west. Then he said, "Here we are, the world-famous Platform 276!"

He brought the hover jet over the platform of an abandoned oil derrick a hundred-fifty miles southwest of the Keys. It was rebuilt into a nautical theme covered with Greek statues between jumping dolphins. There were around thirty hover jets parked on the deck and at least that many boats tied up to the docks around the base of the derrick. She noticed a fishing charter boat service on the far end of the derrick that looked like it had a half dozen boats. There was a huge sailfish over the entryway of the elevator. He escorted her to the entrance, which was a glass elevator taking them straight down into the sea, where there was a glass-enclosed restaurant on the floor of the Gulf, which was the shape of a sunken submarine.

The windows were over a foot thick but were crystal clear, and you could see fish swimming in every direction around a nautical scene that resembled the Greek Acropolis. The ocean was lit up with a backdrop of a wall of bubbles while there were schools of every type of multicolored fish swimming around—from groupers to tuna to schools of shrimp, making a colorful kaleidoscope of sea life and an ever-moving seascape. The ocean floor was covered with lobsters, crabs, and clams sitting on coral outcroppings. The fish were being fed by multiple divers in different colored neon suits with trained dolphins swimming through the scene, herding the different schools of fish through a series of tunnels and arches. It was as if they were at the bottom of a giant aquarium. This had to be the most charming and beautiful place she had ever seen.

"How did you find out about this place?"

He just laughed and said, "You forget—I've lived my entire life on the Gulf oil rigs, and I sold this one to the owner. Here he is now. Terrance Jasmine, you have any fresh fish? I want to introduce you to my lovely friend, June Darling."

Terrance Jasmine was a large black man who had a wide girth and an even wider smile, with a shaved head and two laughing brown eyes. He was a Creole from New Orleans who grew up in the Cajun restaurants where he learned to cook. He brought his family recipes to their customers, who became followers of his uniquely spicy seafood, chowder, and gumbo. By the time he was thirty, he had his own restaurant, and within three years, he had one of the busiest places in New Orleans. That is when he had the idea for the Platform restaurant on the bottom of the Gulf.

"Welcome to the Submariner Restaurant, Ms. Darling. You are aptly named! How did you end up with this long, tall drink of water? A beautiful lady like you can do a lot better than him!" His laugh filled the room.

"I saw your speech tonight, Steven, and what an inspiration! You gave those UN dictators a piece of your mind and told them who and what Texas is about. Makes me wish I built this off Texas with the rest of your freedom lovers, but unfortunately, I have too much invested here, and you cannot just move an oil derrick. Tonight, my brother with another color, whatever you want is on me!"

"Thank you so much, my dear friend, but I insist on paying. Anybody who can cook swordfish like you deserves to be rewarded for it. Besides, who is going to pay the divers? They all look a bit skinny!"

Terrance's face lit up, and he laughed. "Well, even God knows you can afford it, my friend. Come sit down and let me make you the best meal you two have ever tasted. Now, Miss Darling, tonight, the diet is off. I am going to fix you some food that when you taste it, you will wish you were fat like me. My momma was the best cook in New OR-lins, and she taught me everything she knew. Welcome!"

June enjoyed the fun teasing and responded, "You don't have to worry about me. My daddy is a preacher, and he told me two things: you do not order fish in Omaha or order steak in New Orleans. I think I will have the swordfish and gumbo."

"Ah, *cherie* can eat and laugh! I like her already. You better grab this one, Mr. Moses, before she spits the hook. She is what we say in the Keys, a woman with a spirit that ignites your soul's fire."

Now Steven became a bit tongue-tied. "There you go, my friend. That's what I have kept telling her, but she just won't hear of it. She seems to think we must get to know each other or something? I just think she's waiting for something better to come by."

June just sat down and smiled contently.

"I'm sorry if we embarrassed you."

"Not at all, taking me here is amazing. Terrance really is a sweetheart, and he has a special restaurant. How often can you say you have eaten seafood with the fishes on the bottom of the sea?"

"Not very often, this is one of the best-kept secrets in the Gulf and one of the hardest restaurants to get to. We are one-hundred-fifty miles southwest of the Keys, and the only way to get here is by air or boat. It's always filled. People who have found out about Platform 276 come back as often as they can. Not only is it a unique dining experience seventy feet underwater, but Terrance is one of the best chefs anywhere. What more could you ask for?"

Their waitress arrived at their table with the first course of seaweed-wrapped shrimp and scallops, spicy calamari, crayfish tails along with some Creole bread, and a cup of jambalaya with garlic croutons. She spoke in a thick Jamaican accent, "Hello, my name be Charlene, your waitress for the evening. Mr. Terrance says to enjoy our specialty for an appetizer, which is our Submariner Seafood Starter. He says to enjoy the chowder, and your fresh swordfish will be swimming by shortly."

June laughed as she left and looked at Steven in a serious manner. "Steven, I have to tell you something. I recently received a grant at the university to write a paper about this battle between Texas and the UN, and I wanted you to know about it."

"Really? That's amazing, and what perfect timing! Texas needs someone to explain our side of the story, and we understand the New York and world media will only tell the UN side and make us out to be the villains. We need someone to professionally document these historic events. Maybe you can turn it into a book. How did you get this opportunity, and should I be careful what I say around you from now on?"

She laughed at that. "No, of course not. This is going to be an academic record of our history and documenting the events as they occur. The university approached me to do this since a company donated enough to cover my sabbatical and expenses. That's the reason I was at the speech today and had no idea you would see me from the stage, let alone come up and find me. Did your company give the grant to the university?"

"I have no idea. If you're asking if I paid it, the answer is no, but I have no idea if Moses Industries or one of the affiliates did since that is not part of my responsibilities or knowledge. Although I do enjoy the idea of having you writing this paper and having you around, it certainly brightens up the room."

"Ha-ha! Aren't you clever, Steven Moses? How seriously do you think the UN is about forcing you to join the Union?"

"I honestly don't know, but we do know they're going to push it as far as they can to get the tax dollars. They're having serious financial and worldwide control problems due to the ongoing recession, so they're going to attempt to get us to join. Whether they're willing to use military options to make that happen is anyone's guess. I pray they don't. What do you think?"

"Me? Why does it matter what I think? I have nothing to do with this."

"Apparently, you do, and who could possibly know more about the subject than you right now? I want to know what you think will happen."

"Well, if you need to know, I think they will push it to the military solution and make Texas submit to their authority. They have too much to lose if you were to successfully stand up to them. What would stop other countries from breaking away from their control and taxing authority if you defied them and succeeded? I think this is a very dangerous situation and is one of the main reasons I want to write about it. This may be the decisive battle between capitalism and communism, and we have no idea how it will turn out. This is the ultimate dream for a journalist—to record a great battle between two economic theories. Who could ask for more?"

"That is the main reason you want to write about this. I feel slighted. Now look at us here, we are at one of the most romantic restaurants in the world, and all we do is talk about the potential end of the world. Don't you like the surroundings or the company? Did anybody tell you your eyes sparkle like green pearls underwater?"

Her face lit up, and the twinkle in her eyes brightened in their intensity. He had not felt like this since Sandy and he were dating in college. Why does she remind him so much of Sandy and how is he falling so fast and so hard?

"I bet you use that line on all the girls you bring here," she said teasingly.

"Nope, the only other girl I brought here is my Executive Secretary, and it was with the entire Board of Directors, so I never got a chance to use it. Not to mention her husband would make hamburgers of me if I did. I really am glad you came here, and I really enjoy it when we have time together. And, yes, I know we barely know each other, but it just seems like we've known each other longer than we have."

June smiled a very warm smile as her eyes reignited, and she simply said, "Yes, I know, I feel the same way."

Charlene returned with Terrance, and their dinners of swordfish stuffed with rock crab served on rice pilaf and garnished with lemon, mango, and parsley served on a banana leaf. It smelled and looked mouth-watering. Terrance walked over and said, "I hope this dish proves to you, cherie, you're not eating fish in Omaha."

"Terrance, Jasmine, this doesn't look anything like Omaha, and you proved that my daddy was wise beyond his years."

Terrance laughed and clapped his hands as the lights inside dimmed to candlelight, and multicolored bubbles began falling from the ceiling. The stage lights on the Greek stage brightened. The divers began line dancing to the "Yellow Rose of Texas" while the dolphins were doing an intricate choreography swimming in and out of the columns, and the stage was immersed with the multicolored schools of fish. As the song ended, the divers all lined up with neon signboards reading, "Don't mess with Texas!

Terrance just laughed and loudly said, "Ladies and gentlemen, I would like you all to welcome my good friend and Texan, Steven Moses, and his lovely guest, Professor June Darling." The restaurant erupted as the diners stood in unison to give them an ovation.

June leaned over to Steven and whispered, "Is it always this friendly down here?

RESOLUTION 2033-311

Secretary-General Polentas sat at the head of the conference table with her cabinet as they prepared for the Texas Conference coming the following week. She was wearing a cream-colored business suit with a large eagle broach on the left side of her chest. Her cabinet consisted of the ambassadors to Nigeria and Iran, as well as Great Britain, the United States, Canada, Germany, Russia, Japan, and China. There were another fifteen countries sitting in virtual seats who could not attend.

She opened the meeting: "United Nations Ambassadors, thank you for your time. I am so glad to have you attend this especially important meeting. As you know, we are trying to negotiate a treaty with the Republic of Texas, and so far, they have resisted all our offers. I hope you know the importance of their participation with our Union of Nations.

"It is critical that they no longer exploit the world's resources and assets without having to contribute anything back to those of us who maintain these assets and protect their profits. This is a great financial burden for the UN, and as everyone here knows, we can no longer afford to pay for their use of our infrastructure uncompensated.

"We also insist they become a better world neighbor and stop exploiting the air and water resources we have tried so hard to maintain. They have not allowed a world monitoring of their pollution levels or water standards, and this potentially affects all of us and especially their neighbors in Mexico and the United States. We demand they begin allowing our inspectors to verify the implementation and verification of their industrial production.

"Our final requirement is that they also verify the fair wage resolution we instituted in 2029 to protect the workers from exploitation. We have had reports of Texas companies not complying, and we do not find it equitable to the rest of the world neighborhood and challenge the questionable exploitation of workers. We need to know they are paying a fair living wage and that those who are working have a wage that allows them dignity and value in their neighborhoods. We believe a good working environment is a worker's right and not a benefit. These issues, we are afraid, are human rights violations and demand they comply immediately.

"We believe these are fair requests for a country using our world banking and transportation facilities as well as becoming a responsible world neighbor. This will make the United Nations a more effective manager of the world economies helping all our countries become stronger together. We can obviously assist some of the more needy countries to help keep the peace in those regions. We need to be unified in these requests, so they know they are isolated in the world community."

The first to respond was the German Ambassador. "Madam Secretary-General, we are in complete agreement. We are good business partners with the Republic of Texas since we export car and truck engines to them, and they export shiploads of refined oil products to us. As valuable a trading partner as they are, we understand and support the position of the United Nations. If we do not work as a unified world, then many nations will suffer while others like Texas will have unfair advantages. We need to level the resources and eliminate the advantages for all nations."

Next was the Congo Ambassador. "Since we found our oil reserves five years ago, which are estimated to be one of the top five finds in the world, we have been one of the top suppliers of the Texas refineries. They have always treated us fairly and are a good trading partner. We have been able to feed our people, but there is much work to be done in our region. There is only so much we can do, and many countries can use additional United Nations help. For this reason, we will support the UN resolution 2033–311 to bring Texas into the world community."

Finally, the Ambassador to China spoke. "Madam Secretary, we support your resolution with some reservations. We are Texas's largest customer for petroleum products, and our economy demands a consistent supply of these products. We have a complicated relationship with them as they are both a supplier and a customer as well as a competitor for many of our businesses which choose to relocate there. They have many advantages over our country, of which their lack of a world business tax is an attractive benefit. We would be very well pleased to have them begin to pay a tax like ours and the rest of the world. The concern we have is if this were to become a protracted negotiation or action. We cannot afford to have our gas and oil supply cut off for an extended period. Has the Madam Secretary or her military advisers discussed this possibility and how to move things along in a timely manner?"

"Ambassador Wong, yes, we have discussed this as this has been a common concern for many of our member countries, including the US. We plan on putting a naval and air blockade in place to stop all shipping and transportation, which we believe will have an immediate impact on the Texas economy. We believe this will end either immediately or certainly in a matter of weeks. We have estimated they will be feeling this disruption immediately and will bring them to the negotiating table very quickly. In the event we need more aggressive measures, we will look at those on a case-by-case basis."

"Madam Secretary, if this lasts longer than a couple of months, many of the less-developed countries could start running out of fuel, and that could bring critical hardships to their people. Many of our member countries can barely keep their industries producing now, so what would happen if they ran out of petroleum products due to this disruption? They could have a hard time feeding their people. This action could lead to mass starvation. We need assurances that this will not be a long and protracted war. Texas is a powerful country that can sustain itself for a long time. Much longer than our countries, especially with the economic disruption this war could inflict on the entire world. They are the suppliers of our basic energy needs, and this could harm us in ways we are not foreseeing. I simply hope Madam Secretary has thought through all the different scenarios. Thank you for your time, Madam Secretary, and my fellow ambassadors."

Secretary Polentas finished. "We have discussed all of your concerns, which are also our concerns, and we believe we have the basis of a plan that would require a short action to bring this to a positive resolution. We thank you for all of your time, and we welcome all of your suggestions."

"Rattler to air command. We are in hot pursuit of a bogey pilot who has crossed the Texas border and is now returning north to the border at Mach 4.8. We will be crossing the Oklahoma border in two minutes and request your approval to stay on our target outside Texas airspace."

"That's a negative, Rattler. We do not want to commit an international incident, which could be considered an act of war. We can't afford to be pulled into this type of action, which could have unintended casualties. Break from your pursuit, and that is an order!"

"Roger that. What is going on through this corridor? Did you get any computer or engine signatures from our sensors?"

"Negative, Rattler. Whatever they are using can avert our sensors with no trace. Our tech guys have no idea what they are using or how they are doing it. You can bet they will figure it out; it will just take some time." Terry Thomas knew he had to get back to headquarters and check his data.

He understood the cat-and-mouse game of testing their defenses, but to cross the border is a highly risky tactic if they were to get caught. They had to be doing more than that, but what could it possibly be? Were they planting sensors of their own or photographing areas they couldn't get from satellite? It just didn't make sense. All he knew was he would like to give that guy another shot and even things up.

"Hello, Professor Darling, this is the Texas Ranger. Do you have a minute?"

"Yes, hello? Why do you sound upset?"

"The authorities have declared martial law for the upcoming UN summit. They are cracking down on all the freedom groups and especially ours. The city has become a fortified prison camp, and they are declaring curfew at sundown and rounding up everyone they can. They have built an electronic web that can detect anything or anyone moving for over a square mile around the building. Anybody caught moving around is immediately being jailed, and if they belong to the Texas Christ Church, they are being sent upstate. Are you coming to the summit? I would like to meet with you if possible."

"Yes, I am coming with the Moses group and the Texas delegation since I am recording this event as a journalist. How can we meet?"

"Don't worry, my people can make it happen. Are you going to be staying in the same hotel as the Moses group?"

"I don't think they will be spending the night. They are taking the Lone Star Air shuttle and flying around Florida, which only takes thirty minutes. I'm a bit anxious flying on that rocket—it sounds terrifying."

"Sounds like an amazing ride. I will have my people contact you inside the UN to pass on what's happening in the city. It's too dangerous to transmit these files to you electronically, but we will find a way to get you the videos and pictures we have explaining the conditions here and what we've found out about the gangs. There are some direct links we need to show you. You'll find much of what we're finding very interesting. I must go before they trace where I am. We will reach you when you arrive. God bless you, and don't 'Mess with Texas!'"

"God bless you, Ranger, and God bless Texas!"

Steven met his team at Moses Tower before sunrise to get prepared for their day at the UN General Assembly. They would meet President Stewart and his team along with June at Texas Space for the flight to New York. His prep team had been working all night, analyzing what they believed would be the proposals the assembly would have for Texas. They expected the worst since the worldwide recession had brought the tax revenues down every year for the last five years. His secretary Debra Jenkins brought in Drake and June Darling as well as the catering staff with a breakfast buffet for the staff and his team.

Debra asked, "Well, Steven, is this the young lady everybody has been talking about? I'm so glad to meet you, Professor Darling. I hope you have a great flight to New York. That big bird is only terrifying for the first twenty minutes, and then it's like falling out of the sky in a brick. Other than that, there is nothing to worry about."

June laughed nervously and looked over at Steven, who locked his gaze on her as he said, "I hope your flight down here was good. It's not as bad as she says, and you may just enjoy it if you like that kind of thing. We have a big day, so get something to eat, and we'll be on our way. Have you been to New York lately?"

"Not lately, I worked for the *New York Times* before they went bankrupt and haven't been there for five years. After they reorganized, I went on my own and earned my doctorate at Columbia like every other journalism professor. I knew the city pretty well. It's changed since I was there — and not for the better. I've never flown anywhere near those speeds before, so I don't know if I can eat; I'm pretty nervous."

"Oh, don't be; it's like flying any other plane, it just takes off a lot faster, and we won't be going out of the atmosphere on this flight. Normally, we wouldn't use it for a short hop like this, but we really don't have anywhere safe to spend the night in New York, so we may as well fly in and out. We're not exactly going to have the Welcome Mat put out for us. It's a half-hour flight, and we will be over the ocean the entire time to avoid sound corridors and keep with US sovereignty laws. You should get a bite; this is going to be a really long day, and you will be needing to keep your strength."

They flew down to Houston Space with Drake and Dave Scott, who would focus on the oil issues they would be discussing. After they met with President Stewart, Vice President Chapman, and Senate Leader

Gerald Crockett, they boarded the ramjet shuttle and prepared for their flight. June settled in next to Steve and held his hand as the booster rockets fired and blasted them into the sky. Once they were ten miles up, the booster's shut down, and then they could feel the power of the ramjet taking it to the speeds she had read about as she was pushed into her seat, making her stomach a bit queasy.

She squeezed Steven's hand for all she was worth as terror rushed through her veins, and then it became exciting beyond description. They were gaining speed and altitude as she watched the earth turn from a flat horizon into a round globe; then, the engines just stopped, and they silently glided back to earth. She had never imagined what the earth would look like at these heights, and as soon as she was amazed by the power and speed, they were preparing to land in New York. It was a breathtaking flight; even though it felt like going to Dallas, it was so short.

They landed at La Guardia, and now it was perfectly named since it was an armed camp. The entire airport was walled with guard towers every hundred yards armed with laser tasers to keep the gangs out. They could hear the gun battles being fought across the river and smoke rising from a few buildings in downtown Manhattan. They flew separate hover jets for security because of all the gangs waiting for their arrival and were inside the UN in another thirty minutes, being escorted to a conference room next to the assembly. Everybody opened their files in preparation for their presentation.

President Stewart began the meeting. "I don't think I have to tell you this room is not secure, so we need to keep our conversations very generic, and let's not disclose too much. We all know what we're going to be saying, but we need to be prepared with our speeches. We're going to basically follow the same format as our speeches to the Texas assembly but will have to focus on informing the people who will be watching around the world. They have given me a half hour to speak, and Steve will have fifteen minutes. Then the secretary-general will give a speech, followed by President Chambers. We'll then have a chance for rebuttal, and the entire chamber will begin the debate with our team answering their questions. We need to pray for guidance and strength before we go into this chamber. Any questions?"

Steven spoke first, "Yes, David, this is going to be a very high-stakes battle between Texas and the United Nations. You know they are looking at more taxes than any other country. How hard do we want to hit them in this address?"

"Well, Steve, like we have said in our past meetings, they need to know that we are not ready to back down, so why shouldn't we tell them just that. There is really no point in pulling punches since, at this point, it's likely their minds are already made up. We can hopefully reach one or two countries who can stop this with a veto, or we will simply have to go to the next step, whatever that could be. Is everybody ready? Let's pray. Will you lead us, Steve?"

Terry Thomas was meeting with the technology geeks to find out how these bogeys were still crossing the borders undetected. These laser detectors had some of the most advanced technology Texas Instruments in partnership with the most advanced engineering companies, could develop, which should not be able to compromise their laser detection grid, yet it did.

Bill Branson was an immigrant from Florida who had graduated at the top of his class at MIT and became a head engineer for a defense contractor in Miami. After immigrating to Texas four years ago, he installed and updated the laser detection pods as well as the transmission system to the central computers. He and his team of technicians have developed the most sophisticated system in the world, yet somebody has invented a stealth system to counter his units.

"Terry, we've been going over the data, and not only is there no record of the intruder, but there is also a twenty-second blank spot on the devices. We can't tell if there's an override on the device or if it's in the transmission back to headquarters. This means one of two things:

either they have a countermeasure on their aircraft, which can shut our detection devices down, or we have somebody compromising our system. Either way, it's serious, but the second is obviously more concerning since it would mean somebody in our tech program is compromising our security for some reason."

"Is there any way to determine which it is?" Terry asked.

"Not really at this time," Branson replied. "We're analyzing the units to see if they had shut down, and so far, we see no evidence of that. But we're not sure whether they actually shut down or were compromised by a stealth jamming system. We have another problem that is more serious, though. As we began checking these detection units and the other units around the country, we began finding the same thing on others. It appears there are a number of corridors that have been compromised, and we've been invaded by these aircraft for at least the last twelve months—and numerous times without detection."

"Where are they coming in, and where are they going?"

Branson continued, "They are coming in from two areas in the north, one on the east, and one on the west. We figure they're not coming across the south due to all the traffic that could detect them or perhaps see them. They're coming through the least populated areas so they won't be heard or seen, which are also the most difficult to spread our laser detection pods tightly enough, so it's easier for them to compromise."

"We need to step up our patrols in those areas and upgrade our weapons to, hopefully, get a shot at one of these bogeys," Terry offered.

"We also need to find out if we're being compromised by our own people, so we need to compartmentalize all our systems so no one can know the entire system in order to compromise it. Other than myself and my immediate staff, nobody will understand how and what the different pieces are to our defensive system or how they fit together." .

"I agree," Terry nodded in agreement.

Branson continued, "We'll need to only report to each other, and I'll coordinate with those in our departments who need to set up the counter-measures. If there is a mole, we can't let him know we're looking. He's obviously good enough to be able to compromise the system without detection, so if we let too many people know about these jets, he may disappear, and we wouldn't find who he's working for and why. There's also a real possibility there is no mole, and they've found how to electronically manipulate our defenses or are infiltrating our border and manually compromising them. The odds of either of those are slim with our counter-measures, but any counter-measure can be compromised by someone, so anything is possible."

Terry asked, "Do you think there's a possibility they were coming here and dropping surveillance electronics inside our country? Is it possible they could have been on some type of spy mission inside our borders rather than simply testing our defenses?"

"That's exactly what I've been thinking, Terry. Nothing else makes sense, but we have no idea what they were doing. We're looking for electronic spying devices, although if they're preparing for war, they may not get activated until later when they need them. Either way, it's the old needle-in-a-haystack to find them, even when they're running, let alone if they're sitting dormant."

The UN chamber was filled beyond capacity with ambassadors and dignitaries from around the world. This was the largest assembly since the decertification of Israel as a nation vote two years ago. Bringing the newly formed Texas into the United Nations was as critical an endeavor as any in its history. The Texas delegation was seated at the front on the left in a dignitary box, while the UN leaders were seated in the front, facing the assembly. A silence came over the crowd as Secretary-General Polentas strode up to the lectern.

"My fellow Ambassadors, Senators, Texas delegation, and citizens of the world, thank you for coming to this historic world assembly. Since their secession and formation as a nation, we believe we have given the Republic of Texas ample time to become economically viable before they

The Republic of Texas

were offered membership to this world union. We are here today to debate and vote on United Nations Resolution 2033–311, which is the Republic of Texas membership ratification. They have been a valuable member of the economic world, and now it is time for them to become a valuable member of our world organization. We look forward to welcoming them as full United Nations members. With that designation, they will receive all the benefits that go with that membership, such as protection and settlement of disputes throughout the world in the World Court.

"As a nonmember of the UN, they have been able to make use of our military protection and commerce infrastructure without having to contribute to the expenses of those services. They have been allowed to ship their products around the world using many of our port facilities without having to pay the costs of keeping those ports and shipping lanes open. This was understandable as they were a new nation and not yet economically stable. However, now they are not only viable but have become one of the leading financial forces in the world and need to begin sharing the UN expenses.

"In addition, we as citizens of the world need to be environmentally aware of our natural resources such as clean air and water. This has become a burden to their neighboring countries, which have been breathing their pollution and drinking their polluted water both on the surface and throughout the various aquifers. We will help you to attain and maintain our standards to help you stay within the UN-agreed drinking water standards to protect the earth from excessive pollutants and contaminants.

"It is our duty as citizens of the world to protect our children and grandchildren from dirty air and water, so we need to install and maintain the UN environmental team to help make sure their industries are not polluting the worldwide air and water inventories. We will need to monitor and maintain their ocean platforms and production facilities to make sure the quality of the seawater is maintained to worldwide United Nations standards. Our ocean life demands a quality of water be maintained to the strictest measurements as it is throughout the member nations. We do not have to remind anybody of the great 2028 Brazilian spill and the hundreds of square miles of destruction it caused to both fish and wildlife. If that were to occur in the Gulf, there would be millions of people affected and a biological disaster of epic proportions.

"Texas will have an equal voice in all of these issues from the moment they become a member of this body. They will be allowed on the UN Security Council, which would give them a veto vote on any military actions we were undertaking as well as many UN resolutions. They would be allowed an exemption seat on any committee to which they are nominated or elected. This would allow them a voice on the Energy Committee or a Commerce Committee to give them a real influence in the UN government.

"Texas would have full voting privileges immediately, which would make them a powerful voice in the world. Their citizens would be immediately covered under the UN Health Care Program as well as the Fair Workers' Living Wage Program and our World Social Security Retirement Program. We have had the most successful health care program in the history of the world: we are covering seven billion people with quality health care with little or no cost to the patient. They would have the option of using ours or their programs, depending on their preference.

"We are offering Texas an interim discounted transitional membership that we offer to our new members. It will initially be fifteen percent of gross profits from their industries for the first year and increase over five years to our full membership of thirty-five percent. This will allow them time to adjust their industrial and governmental responsibilities while they transition into full membership. The obvious advantages are the military and social protections as well as the added benefit of having most of their governmental duties being handled by our UN continental offices. We are looking forward to a long and prosperous partnership. Let me speak for everybody in this family of Nations; we would be honored to add the Republic of Texas as one of our new members. Thank you."

As the Secretary-General sat down, the President of the General Assembly, Uganda Ambassador Mohamed Achmed Julestuli, stood and walked to the podium.

"It is my honor to open this session to discussion, and the first person on the forum to speak is the president of the Republic of Texas, President David Stewart."

President Stewart made his way from the tables on the floor up the steps to the podium and began to address the over two thousand dignitaries assembled in the large hall.

"Secretary-General Salinas Margarita Polentas, President Julestuli, assembled Ambassadors, dignitaries, worldwide viewers, and fellow Texans. I come here in both humility and honor that this body would consider us for this invitation. We, as Texans, are honored and proud you would offer us this position in as short a time as we have been a country. We have discussed this offer at length, and I am here to say we must respectfully decline your generous offer. We as Texans need to keep our sovereignty and economic freedom from outside intervention that would have to be mandated through the United Nations Charter. No country has been forced to accept membership of the UN before, and we do not believe this is the time or situation that requires this precedence.

"We as a country would be willing to provide for our own protection of our shipping lanes and port facilities with our own ships and weapons to protect us from sea-going pirates and other dangers. We would even be willing to pay the UN a fee for that protection on the open seas from rogue countries attempting to hijack ships like we have been victims of in the recent past. We would even be willing to work out an agreeable fee for those costs of sea transportation for our goods to cross those sea lanes, so we would be willing to drop the maritime protections and costs.

"The people of the Republic of Texas have met and voted on this measure in its Congress and find it both restrictive and excessive, which compromises our sovereignty as a country. We are a deeply independent country which is a major reason why we seceded from the United States.

We feel the entrance into the UN would hinder our independence as well as our ability to maintain our economic freedom, creativity, and viability.

"Our senate met and discussed this resolution at length and has unanimously voted to reject it at this time and to keep our Republic an independent country. We are very satisfied with our system of government, which values small, localized governments rather than a massively large, centralized government, which is why our federal government is purposely weakened compared to our local county officials.

"We have organized our country so that the local municipalities make decisions on where to spend their resources and how to tax and spend them rather than from a central capital like Austin. We feel the local officials have a better idea of how to use their funds on local items which are in their jurisdiction and expertise rather than someone a few hundred miles away. To turn our control over to a worldwide government in New York City goes against our basic form of governance.

"The final issue is your elimination of the Christian Church's right to freedom of speech and religion. Over eighty percent of Texans are God-fearing Christians, and the churches are a primary partner of our welfare system. Texans, in general, not only worship in the church, but the church is a place where people come to be fed both physically and spiritually. Many of our food and poverty programs are directly attached to the churches in Texas, which we consider a one-stop shop for the soul.

"Our churches not only feed the stomach, but they heal the heart through the salvation of Jesus Christ while offering counseling as well as every type of health care assistance. The church offers job search and family guidance to completely heal the person in need and get him back on his feet. Your incitement speech regulations would put our pastors' jobs at risk with their biblical beliefs and destroy our social safety net to be replaced with the UN government programs, which turn people into wards of the state. We believe our churches are far more effective and have the results to prove it.

"For these reasons, our congress voted to respectfully reject United Nations Resolution 2033-311. My friend and CEO of Moses Enterprises, Steven Moses, would like to address the economic issues regarding our decision. Thank you for your time."

There was polite yet sparse applause that spread across the assembly in response to his remarks. As Steven rose to address the General Assembly, he looked up in the balcony where he saw June applauding his upcoming remarks.

He glanced over the United Nations General Assembly and thought how a kid could go from working on an oil rig spitting chaw to this moment. He knew God had guided his path as well as his father and mother's encouragement, who taught him to do everything the right and honest way. Now he was about to give a speech to the entire world about one of the most critical issues to avoid a world war between Marxism and free-market capitalism.

"Madam Secretary-General Polentas, General Assembly President Julestuli, United Nations Ambassadors, distinguished guests, and people of the world, it is in humility we come to you tonight. We have become a powerful nation in a brief period, and it is our hope and prayers every country in this assembly could become economically everything and more than we are. We have accomplished this by using our resources, hard work, and ingenuity to become one of the most powerful countries in the world.

"I am the son of a wildcatter, and through long hours and an innovative patent, my company has been able to recover oil which previously had not been recoverable. This innovation allowed me and my team to build one of the largest oil companies in the world. We believe in giving our customers the best value for their money, and Texas has followed that same path. We are now the largest energy producer in the world, not only in petroleum products but also in electrical generation, as we produce a substantial percentage of the electrical energy for the United States, Mexico, and most of South America. We have developed underwater trunk lines and are now powering Hawaii and, in the future, Japan as well as parts of Africa.

"We look at the world market as one worldwide open-air market. Just like you see in all the old movies or in underdeveloped countries where people put out their wares on a blanket or table and haggle over the prices, so, too, does our marketplace. We have millions of people making millions of transactions every minute of the day, negotiating the value of a product or service. Each person makes those decisions without the help or interference of a government entity which in turn makes those transactions easier and more efficient and by what those people decide the good is worth.

"By shrinking the size and power of the government, we increase the power and creativity of the individual. This is the basis of how the free-market economy works—by allowing the individual freedom to invent, develop, and market his products, then let the market decide what is good or bad as well as what is a fair price. He will have to go against someone trying to get the same order, so he will have to keep his prices in line or find ways to make his pricing more competitive. We have used this basic concept to become the world leader in energy products as well as many related industries.

"The key requirement to this form of economics is honor, trust, and integrity. Unless you can trust the person you are dealing with to provide or pay for what he says he will do, you cannot have a free market. A free market requires that trust, or it all falls apart. Without trust, you must bring in lawyers or more levels of government to make sure everyone will perform to the levels they claim they will. In our case, if we agree to provide a million barrels of oil by a certain date, we are required to deliver it by that date at the agreed-on price, and the customer is required to pay for it in full.

"Another large part of Texas's success is the low levels of taxation and regulation required from our government. We work together as a partnership, since in Texas we believe that the government that works best is one that works least. This gives our citizens the freedom to use their own independence and ingenuity to become the best they can be. This makes for a fertile environment for business to grow and expand into the economic success Texas has become. This is a unique relationship that is more fertile for a healthier economy and stronger government because the revenues go to the local municipalities where funds are distributed much more efficiently, directly to the people.

"Our businesses would have a tough time surviving, let alone thriving, if we were required to pay the UN tax of thirty-five percent on top of our present tax structure. We would also lose our ability to work efficiently with the regulations you have on our class of industries. We already have some of the cleanest plants in the world, but your regulations are unclear and excessive, in our view, and would adversely restrict our ability to develop and produce our products. This would not only be an added burden on us but also an added hidden cost for all the countries that import our products due to higher costs being added to our pricing. This would negatively affect every country in the world and especially the weaker countries, as our energy price increases would hurt them the most.

"We have the most innovative and generous wages and benefits of any country in the world. We allow our workers and management to become the best they can possibly be on an individual basis. Our two-year waiting list for immigration is testament to these wage structures. The World Union would destroy our ability to maintain our pay and benefit programs as well as divide workers from management. This relationship is one of the main factors making us the most productive and competitive workforce anywhere. We cannot allow the World Union to destroy what we have built between worker and management over these years.

"Our economic advancements and business models have allowed us the lowest unemployment rates of any nation as well as the highest levels of income. This has allowed us to become the most generous country in the world as we have come to the aid of all natural and man-made disasters for any country and provide nearly as much assistance as the United Nations by ourselves. I only point this out to bring us to our worship of God, as we are a Christian nation. We are deeply religious and believe in helping our brothers and sisters no matter who or where they are. Over seventy percent of Texans are regular attendees who consider themselves conservative, Spirit-filled Christians."

Steven looked around to see how his speech was being received and searched up into the balcony to try to spot June, only to see an empty seat. He expected she was coming down to join them or stepped out for a minute as he continued,

"We believe all nations and people are born free and independent as sovereign countries. We have provided not only some of the strongest economic industries, but they are also good stewards of their resources. We have exceeded all our targets in clean air and water to provide a clean and healthy environment for our citizens. All our industrial discharges are monitored and open for review on the company websites twenty-four hours a day for anyone's inspection. Texans are excellent managers of our resources and are conservationists for both the water and air quality. We are not polluting the air in any measurable amounts that would ever reach across our borders to the US or Mexico.

Finally, as to the protection provided by the UN for our shipping lanes. We as a business community would be willing to either provide our own protection or assist the UN in their protection with our assets as we develop them. Our preference would be to purchase the protection from the countries we do business with on a country-by-country basis but would be open to purchasing that protection from the United Nations as a separate revenue for the UN. We believe this is something that can be worked out while we are allowed to stay independent of the UN and keep our sovereignty, which we value more than life itself. I thank you for your time and ask that you consider our arguments thoughtfully. God bless you, and God bless Texas."

THE GREAT DEBATE

June Darling had received a call from the Texas Ranger to meet a girl in the entrance restroom on the first floor of the UN. She had no idea how the girl would be able to get inside the compound and did not ask.

As she entered the restroom, she was met by a young woman named Susan Bennett, who took her to the handicapped stall. Once inside the stall, she opened a hidden door that went into the catacombs of the UN building and eventually into the network of tunnels below the building. Once they were down in the habitat tunnels, she was met by a group of men who escorted them outside the compound and up to a street where a waiting convoy of around ten vehicles picked them up. She didn't know if they were armed but assumed that they were. Susan warned her that even with these men escorting her, they could not protect her from the larger, more organized gangs or the police who were looking for the Texas Christ Church.

The first thing she noticed when they left was the sound of gunshots all around the car and the acrid smell of smoke and rotting flesh. She had no idea where they were coming from or what their targets were, but she could tell they were both close and in the distance in every direction. It sounded like a jungle war zone. She also saw the bodies hanging from the lamp posts throughout the city. They were of all ages and sexes, and you could see entire families hanging with their signs attached to their chests. Some were hanged with stretched-out arms.

"Why are all these people being hanged? Is this the retribution gangs that are lynching people because they are bank executives or business owners? These are the most horrific scenes I have ever seen," she cried as she recorded the video on her handheld computer.

A man in the front seat wearing a black ski mask turned around and said, "Yes, Professor Darling, they are still purging all the capitalists from the economy. These gangs are both organized groups or mercenaries who we believe have coordination from certain groups we are attempting to identify and expose. We think this is the systematic elimination of anybody who is a leader in the business world. We're fighting these gangs using their own tactics and have eliminated several of them and their leaders. We're in a fight for our city, and we want it back."

She recognized the voice, "Are you Ranger?"

"Yes. Pleased to finally meet you, Professor Darling. Excuse the mask, but it's for both our safety. If either of us is captured, you will have nothing of value to give them and will get you out of the situation faster. Believe me, your life is in extreme danger being with us, and the danger factor doubles with me. I'm the Number One prize for the gangs and the UN. Thank you for coming and having the courage to cover this and tell our story."

He gave her some computer pods he said contained all the information she needed to cover the story he had and wanted to take her on an inside tour of New York. She was amazed how old and destroyed the buildings of New York were compared to how she remembered them. Windows were broken out, and doors were laying on the ground with people wandering in and out without the least regard for their maintenance. There were entire walls of skyscrapers that were missing and debris laying in shambles. She saw rats scampering everywhere as the garbage was piled up over two stories in every alley and side street in giant mounds. The smell was sickening from the putrid, oily fragrance of rotting garbage floating in the air.

The convoy rambled down through downtown Manhattan in a tight formation. They obviously knew what they were doing as the lead cars would continually peel off to stop traffic on side streets in case of ambushes. They left the island and headed north toward the Bronx. The intensity of Manhattan lessened, and the gunshots were less frequent, and there were no bodies hanging from any lamp posts except for the occasional gang member who was clearly marked with a cardboard sign attached with a bayonet formed into a cross in his chest.

June looked at Texas Ranger and asked, "Did you kill those men?"

Texas Ranger looked at June and said, "I can't say who killed them. All I can say is they had a better trial than the people they killed. You don't want to know who or why they were killed, except we are in a war, and if anybody is caught in our group, they will likely be hanging from a streetlight within an hour, and that includes you, Professor Darling. When you are in the middle of a war, there will always be the casualties of war.

"I don't know who that gangster is or what he did, but I do know his type. My father was a hardworking stockbroker down on Wall Street, working for Goldman Sachs. He raised us right and never cheated a person in his life. He rose through the ranks specializing in pensions and retirements, helping a lot of people during the collapse to save what they had. Do you know how he was repaid? He was followed home one day eighteen months ago. They broke into his home, beat my mom and sister in front of him, then took them out in the street and hanged them the way they hang Christians. Before they hang them, they stretch a two-by-four behind their neck and over their shoulders, then nail their hands to the ends of the board to form a cross. After he made my father watch them get tortured and hanged, they beat him and hanged him. He was guilty of being a greedy corporate banker. So no, I don't know or care what this guy was caught doing, but you can know he deserved what he received."

June looked him in the eye. "I don't know who you are, and that is a horrible story, but two wrongs do not make a right. No matter how many you kill to get vengeance, it will never bring your family back or make the hurt go away."

"You're right, Professor Darling, but that guy hanging from the lamp post back there won't be attacking the next family he decides is guilty of crimes against the community."

They pulled into a deserted warehouse that said Trimboli's Clothing Warehouse on the side. The lead cars doubled back, blocked the gates, and stayed outside while they went into the warehouse. When they got inside, they found a refurbished building that was turned into an auditorium with a cross at the front and a large sign saying Texas Christ's Church of New York. Texas Ranger motioned for June to come up onto the stage as the crowd stood and applauded his arrival.

Walking to the podium, he spoke with a booming voice as there was no speaker system for fear of the authorities monitoring their services. "Brothers and sisters in Christ, we have just come from the United Nations Building where you all are aware of the debate to force Texas into the Union. We've brought a special guest with us from Texas who is going to tell our story to the outside world. Let me introduce Professor June Darling, who is from the University of Texas—Hook 'em Horns! She's here to report our story."

The entire auditorium gave her a standing ovation as she walked forward and waved.

"Professor Darling, would you mind saying a few words?"

"Why, thank you, I really wasn't expecting to say anything. I guess I would like to say how honored I am to be around people who are willing to take a stand while being persecuted and killed for your faith. In Texas, we have no idea what it would be like to be hunted all the time for being a Christian, and that's what we fear would happen if we were to accept the membership into the United Nations. It is known for its persecution of any religion that strays from their official acceptable language.

"I hope I'm able to tell your story to the world and give the respect each one of your lives deserves. This is a story that needs to be told, and God willing, I will have the skill to provide this vision to the world. Thank you all."

Steven was starting to become concerned about where June could be. It was not like her to just disappear, and this was not the place to do that without telling him or anyone else. His security people told him the last time they saw her, she was talking to someone near the exits at the food courts, and when they looked again, they had disappeared during a rush of people between sessions. They had searched the buildings, and she was not answering her phone. The next speaker was the Ambassador of Iraq and was approaching the dais.

"Madame Secretary General Polentas, General Assembly President Julestuli, United Nations ambassadors, distinguished guests, and citizens of the world. I come to you in humility as a member of this most great assembly of countries. We have a difficult decision to make today. We have heard some persuasive arguments from both Texas and the United Nations. What the people of Iraq understand is the United Nations has been a powerful force for good in this world for nearly one hundred years and, hopefully, will be here long after we have passed this great assembly to the next generation.

"We understand the reservations of Texas to enter into the world community for all of the reasons they have stated. We believe we should give them a grace period to acclimate to their admission and have a sliding scale for their payments and adherence to our world agreements. This would allow them time for their citizens to adapt to our democracy.

"Texas is a good partner and valuable customer of ours since they purchase over sixty percent of our oil. If they could also contribute to the revitalization of their supplying countries' infrastructure, we could more efficiently produce more oil. We have millions of people who are suffering because we cannot produce enough oil to sell on the world market, so many of our people are suffering from hunger and poor roads and services. I know I not only speak for Iraq, but I have toured many of my neighboring countries, and they, too, are suffering from the lack of proper nutrition, education, and medical care. Why should these people suffer when there is so much wealth and luxury in countries like Texas?

"We would also like to address their concern about the control of hate speech in their churches. As many know, we had had our problems in the past over the spreading of hatred from imams inside our Islamic mosques and the violence that occurred when we accepted the hate speech charter. It has been an ongoing struggle, but after our imams accepted the cameras and monitoring regulations, our country has had a decrease in violence of fifty percent over the past five years and is seeing continued improvement. This has been a significant improvement for our citizens and is overwhelmingly supported by our people. I would like to reassure our friends in Texas that after your citizens have accepted the hate restrictions, they will come to appreciate them.

"We hope our friends in Texas will reconsider their opposition to this and look forward to having them as a fellow member of this great union. We look forward to continuing economic prosperity for both countries and expect Texas to be a strong addition to these United Nations. Thank you very much."

President Stewart stepped forward to have a chance to rebut the arguments that were made by the previous speakers. "Madame Secretary General Polentas, General Assembly President Julestuli, United Nations Ambassadors, distinguished guests, and citizens of the world. With all due respect to the speakers who have all spoken, we have heard you and would like an opportunity to discuss it again with our senate, although there is nothing we have heard today that we have not already considered. We believe in a free market that should be allowed to grow and provide jobs and benefits without interference from government management. This not only applies to the UN but our own government is structured in such a way as to give the individual and business as much freedom as possible to follow their own hopes and dreams. To add another level of government from the United Nations only goes against everything Texas—and Texans — believe in.

"We also have an overwhelming issue with the regulating of free speech and the freedom of religion. Unlike many religions around the world, with all due respect, we do not have a problem with violence from our churches or church leaders. What one man considers discussing the societal issues from the Bible, another man considers hate speech. We have read your charter, and there are some genuine issues from the broad interpretations that will limit our churches from preaching and teaching what they believe are the Holy Scriptures from God. We believe the freedom of religion is one of the most basic rights men have, and to limit their worship is an infringement between worshipers and their relationship with God. How do you allow a government to interfere and, in truth, say it has more authority than God? Texans are not going to allow that right to be taken away. I hope you will reconsider UN Resolution 2033–311 and table this proposal. Thank you very much."

Steven was panicking; nobody had heard from June in over four hours, and her phone was not working. The security team checked the cameras, and all they found was her going into one of the restrooms and never coming out. They had later found her earphone in the restroom trash can, so she had no GPS locator. It looked as if she had been kidnapped, but by whom?

Jason Tyler, head of security, was motioning Steven and President Stewart to move to the hover port on the roof. Jason Tyler was six-foot-four and built like a linebacker, although he was a running back in high school before doing two tours of duty in Afghanistan in Special Forces. He had lost track of how many battles and missions he had been on before he began working for international security teams. He was not all that concerned about New York City, but he knew to not take chances when flying exposed over areas that were not controlled militarily. His team was good, but you can only be "so good" when you know there are random hostiles out to kill you. If they were to capture the package, the results would be final and immediate, but he was not planning on them having that opportunity.

"President Stewart, Mr. Moses, we have to get moving. I've talked to the security here, and if she turns up, they will escort her to the airport. It's beginning to get dark, and that will only make things worse from a safety standpoint. We have to get moving, now!"

Texas Ranger was giving a rousing sermon, and the entire crowd was involved, which began giving testimonies of how they have been harassed and threatened by the New York gangs. They told of the most horrific murders, rapes, and beatings of survivors, families, and friends, but the one thing that kept them together was their faith in God.

"Brothers and sisters, we are witnessing a monumental change in history. We are finally seeing neighborhoods fighting back against the murdering gangs and corruption that has taken over the boroughs. We have fought back entire neighborhoods here in the Bronx, Queens, and Long Island and have secured neighborhoods in Manhattan and Newark, but we need to stay strong because they know they must destroy us to completely own New York and the United States. We are the last surviving toehold of America and freedom outside Texas. So far, we have captured, tried, and eliminated over hundred-fifty gang members caught lynching innocent victims.

"Professor Darling has come here despite the dangers and will tell our story about our group and what we stand for. She will tell our story to the world of how a few resistance fighters are willing to risk everything to keep the hope of returning freedom from this oppressive dictatorship. She has risked her safety to come here and record our stories to take them to the world. We have to get moving before their locator drones find out we're here, but let's give another hand for Professor Darling!"

A loud ovation came up as the entire crowd stood and gave another thunderous applause, overwhelming her. The crowd then began to sing "The Star-Spangled Banner" in such an emotional, heartfelt way that one couldn't mistake these were people who knew what each word meant to their lives. The music wafted as the tears flowed in unison. They understood what the author must have imagined and had the same dreams in their minds when they echoed, "The land of the free and the home of the brave."

Suddenly, she heard the crackle of gunfire erupting in the streets behind her, obviously coming from behind the trucks and cars in which they had arrived. The room immediately came to life as all the men

The Republic of Texas

pulled out hidden weapons, running to the windows. Texas Ranger was on an earphone and giving orders to the outside men and showing the ones inside which doors to exit and where to go.

"June, stay down. We're being attacked by the Union Gangs. It's a large, well-armed force, and appears there are several splinter gangs with them. We can get you out through some escape tunnels we have, or if you can call in some help, we can get you to an area out the back that is well secured for a hover jet landing. We don't have any time. Here is a secure phone you can make a call to escape. This may get bloody, and no telling how many they have coming. We need to get you out now. Take this phone, and Susan will take you toward the tunnels."

June was terrified; she had never been this close to gunfire, and she could see and hear the bullets hitting the walls and hear the men screaming in pain. "Let me call Steven and see what he can do." She made her way away from the fighting as the men, and a few of the women went toward it with faces set against the enemy. She dialed the number.

Steven saw the strange number with no ID and answered it, only to hear June's terrified voice and what sounded like a war in the background. She was shouting to him, and he quickly understood she was in trouble.

"Jason, June is in trouble in New York, and we have to go get her. Get your men—let's take my Stallion and get going. It sounds like a war. She just sent me her GPS. We can follow it in the Bronx, but we must go now. I'll fly the hover jet. Let's go."

Jason didn't like the idea of the person he was to protect going on a mission like what he envisioned who didn't have experience in these matters. He was going to be more trouble than help. "Mr. Moses, I can't let you go. Give me the coordinates, and my guys will go get her. We know what we're doing. This is nothing you want to get involved with."

"Jason, I'm paying the bill, and I'm the best hover jet pilot we have. Besides, I am going with or without you, and this is too important for me to sit and wait. Either you let me go — or I go by myself." He jumped into the pilot seat and fired up the Stallion, checking the instruments.

Jason didn't hesitate. "Men, armor up, and let's go. Check your weapons: this LZ is going to be a hornets' nest."

The three men climbed in as the Stallion lifted off, and Steven headed straight for the Bronx, knowing he would be the biggest prize of their lives to have him hanging from a lamp post. Jason was going to make sure they never got that reward.

The river slid behind them as they cruised four hundred feet off the ground flying into the Bronx. They saw the smoke and explosions rising ahead of them and knew this must be what she was talking about. Taking a wide arc, they could see what looked like hundreds of people firing small arms at each other with bodies lying everywhere. Jason had seen skirmishes like this all around the world as one warlord fought another. He never expected to see it in a Borough of New York City, yet here it was. Coming around the back, they pinpointed the beacon and could see people crouched down in a small alcove between some buildings protected by cars and rubble.

The fighters who were attacking the warehouse saw the hover jet and began firing at it, knowing it was in the wrong place at the wrong time. Steven pushed the throttle and pointed the nose straight for the pavement. The gun and laser fire became intense as he headed for the deck like a rock thrown from the sky. Fifty feet from impact, he pulled on the stick and leveled it out, hitting the hover break for all he was worth and hit the ground with a huge bounce and then settled down.

The security team raced to the corners of the hidden alcove and began laying down cover fire on all the surrounding buildings. There seemed to be a hundred men in the windows and roofs of the surrounding buildings, and the hover landing attracted all their attention, knowing there had to be a valuable target they were rescuing.

Steven looked across the alcove and saw June coming his way with a couple of strangers. He jumped out of the hover and ran over to her, hugged her, and swept her up in his arms, protecting her with his body while running back to the Black Stallion. He shoved her into the back covey while jumping over into the pilot seat, revving the jets while motioning for Jason's team to get back in.

Jason and his team straddled their seats, and the outside jump steps continued to fire at every target they saw, hitting mark after mark.

Jason shouted over the confusion, "Go, go, go!"

Steven hit the throttle on both the jump jet and the forward thrust to get as much speed as the hover could produce. It was a trick he learned on some small derrick platforms when he had to fly in severe weather. "Hold on!"

He banked and corkscrewed straight up in a zigzag, making it impossible to be a clear target as every warning light in the cockpit went off at the same time while the men were holding on for all they were worth until he leveled off at a thousand feet, speeding off back to La Guardia, taking less than a minute.

Jason looked over at Steven while securing his rifle. "Any time you need a job as a Special Op's jock, give me a call. That was some fancy flying for a civilian. I don't think I've ever seen a landing or takeoff like that before in one of these. You're a pretty good stick and glad you were there, but don't ever try that again."

Steven smiled and answered, "I had this one juiced up a bit to get a bit more performance out of it for when I'm out on the Gulf. I never really thought it would come in handy when I was being shot at. Guess that Kevlar plating can take a hit or two."

He looked over at June and asked, "What in the world were you doing in the middle of a war, and why did you leave the UN meeting?"

June still looked like she was in shock and quietly answered, "I can't tell you now. We'll talk later."

Thirty minutes later, they were lining up on the Houston Space runway as the shuttle made its final approach from its glide path. June was obviously more relaxed as she returned to Texas after her experience, and Steven was still mystified about what she was doing in the Bronx in the middle of a gunfight.

He grabbed her hand as they landed, and she looked over and smiled while a small tear leaked down her nose, which made his heart skip a beat. "Look, I don't know what you were doing, and it really isn't important. The important thing is you're safe, and we are together. If you don't want to tell me, that's fine. I trust you knew what you were doing. You are in no condition to drive, so let me fly you home, and I will have someone drive your car to your place in the morning."

She smiled and said, "That would be fine. This has been a really exhausting day."

After they landed and got into the hover limo, they dropped June and Steven at Moses Towers, where they got into a company hover jet and flew to Austin while she enjoyed the lights below. "You know this is the most beautiful country on earth and so peaceful. I could not talk when we were with the security guards since I was there to cover a story."

June explained to Steven how and why she was in the Bronx while they left Houston.

He reached over and grabbed her hand again, and she squeezed it as she leaned over and rested her head on his shoulder. He could hear her breath soften as she gently fell asleep from exhaustion while he flew the rest of the way into Austin, taking a long circle as he enjoyed the feeling of her head on his shoulder while her hair cascaded down his chest. Finally, he found her house and parked on her driveway as she was awakened by the landing.

"Are we here? Did I fall asleep? I must have dozed off! I'm so sorry."

He smiled down at her and said, "Don't worry. I kind of enjoyed the feeling of you sleeping on my shoulder. I could get used to that after a while. Let me walk you to your door. We don't want anyone attacking you again."

She let out a small laugh. "Thank you for everything. This was a day I will never forget, and I'm so sorry to drag you into that situation. I had no idea it was going to be that dangerous. Those Christians needed me, and they are some of the bravest people in America. You saved my life, and I really don't know what to say. That was brave and heroic. I was stunned."

"Now, why would you be stunned? I would prefer 'shining white knight,' but 'hero' will work." The moon shimmered off her hair, blinding his eyes with a rainbow-colored sheen while they talked about the day. He looked into her two deep pools of emerald green that swallowed him up like a flower swallowing a bee. Reaching around her small waist, he pulled her to him as she looked up into his eyes as their lips met. It was everything he knew it would be as he found who completed him again. This was more than a kiss, but a possession of two people by the other as they bonded into a ring forming between them. Both of their lives up to that point were past, and this kiss pointed them to the future, which was their new horizon. Then as quickly as it began, the kiss was over, completing the moment.

"Well, good night, June. I will call you in the morning."

"Ah, yeah, call me. Good night, Steven," she said as she fumbled at the code pad, dazed, wobbled, and in shock, knowing this was more than a good night kiss.

Steve hopped back into the hover jet, gave it everything it had, and corkscrewed it into the sky, repeating the maneuver in New York as she smiled and slumped against the door. "What have I gotten myself into?" She reached over to her left forearm and pinched herself twice.

Midnight was a tough hour for any pilot, and Terry Thomas was no different. He was tired, but with all that was happening in New York, he felt something might be happening tonight to test the sensors. Finding the beam diverters next to the pods was a great discovery by the tech crew. Now those bogeys may find it a bit tougher to get through undetected, but they have found out by now and figured a way to counteract it.

He and his wingman, Snakebite, were issued the new craft with the mini-ramjet engines connected to the hover technology. That allowed him to hover as well as travel at Mach 5. In addition, they juiced up the weapons to maximum stun, so whatever they hit would be disabled and must land immediately if they were within thirty miles. He was hoping he would get a chance to use them when suddenly one of the ground monitors lit his screen with an alert and coordinates of a bogey traveling at Mach 4 crossing the border. He saw it as he locked and was counter-locked at the same time. Kicking in the ramjet while firing in unison, he saw the laser attaching to his craft, but the deflectors diverted the beam as he headed for the sky while his beam had a hit on the target. He saw it fall out of the sky, tumbling across a cornfield as the pilot ejected and his power chute motored lazily back across the border.

The adrenaline rush he felt from knocking down his first intruder as a Texan pilot was exhilarating. He had to keep his head in case some of his buddies came in to either attack him or destroy the downed craft. He and Snakebite set up a perimeter and circled until backup arrived to begin recovery and identification of the intruder's craft. As they watched, a charge went off in the wreckage, exploding it in a hundred-yard circle of debris.

June woke up early, got ready to go to work, fixed herself some coffee, and had a grapefruit half with an English muffin for breakfast while she prepared for her day. She had so much to read and analyze with all the data she picked up from Ranger's people she thought it would take weeks to go through. She began searching the news sites to see what she could find out about the attack on the church when the doorbell rang. Looking at the door monitor, she could see it was Steven! What was he doing here? She looked a mess—just out of the shower with wet hair and no makeup.

She spoke into the monitor, "What are you doing here? I wasn't expecting you this morning. Give me a few minutes." She quickly blew her hair and made herself up as best she could without making him wait too long on the porch. She put on a pair of sweats, drug a brush through her hair, swiped on some lipstick and a bit of eyeliner, then met him at the door.

"Good morning, Steven. Did you forget something last night?"

"Yes, I did. I forgot you. I'm not letting you out of my sight from now on, and I came here to pick you up before we attended the States' council meeting."

"What are you talking about? I can go down there myself in a couple of hours and get some work done here and run some errands. I don't have time to go to the council meeting. I haven't had a chance to get ready!"

"Look, June. You want to document this event, and so do I. How close a look inside can you get than by being with me. I'll get you into all the important meetings you want to be in on. Besides, you are one of the most knowledgeable people regarding the United Nations, so you can be a valuable asset for these discussions."

"So, you just want me for my brains. Should I be offended?" she teased.

"Well, your brains are a good start. I think I proved that to you last night, or have you forgotten already? Now, get ready, and let's go. We're meeting President Stewart and the Security Council in ninety minutes. Have you had breakfast yet?"

"That's okay; I already ate."

"I have some things I need to take care of on the hover computer while you change, and we'll take off as soon as you're ready to go."

Steven gave her a quick kiss and a hug as he headed out the door, leaving her head spinning while she stumbled to the bathroom to make that small miracle she had to make happen in fifteen minutes. She just wished she would have taken the time to buy that black pencil skirt she saw last week in Austin.

Terry Thomas and Snakebite had been circling over the crash site all night, waiting for the crash forensic crew to arrive. They would be able to get some identification off the craft and find out who these invaders were and hopefully get into their data and find out why they were coming in. All they needed were some small pieces to find out who was sending these intruders.

He saw the convoy rolling across the horizon off in the distance. They would be here in about thirty minutes, and then they could begin putting this jigsaw aircraft back together again. Hopefully, the computer memory survived the mandatory crash destruction. All these guys needed were a few molecules, and they would be sucking data off the virtual pieces. Still, any government worth their salt knows to turn all their data into dust once the crash was occurring, which was the case with this crash. A spy plane will be especially hard to get a signature, but if anybody can, it's the guys approaching from the south.

A woman's voice broke the still Texan morning dew, "Hello, Captain Thomas, this is Major Morgan. We are about thirty minutes out. Are you the pilot who called in the intruder's crash?"

"Yes, Major, I am the pilot who was attacked and counterattacked, hitting the aircraft and downing it. The pilot was able to escape back across the border with a power-chute, but we have his craft spread across the cornfield underneath me. Do you want me to land and wait for you now?"

"Negative Captain, please keep the area secure. We don't want you to contaminate or compromise any of the evidence. We'll be there in a few minutes. By the way, nice shooting, Captain!"

"Thank you, Major Morgan."

Steven and June walked into the capitol from the VIP hangers directly into the Presidential Wing. There seemed to be more security around the capitol and in the chambers than you would normally notice. They were escorted by two Texas National Guard hovers from ten miles out all the way to the capitol building.

President Stewart's personal secretary, Sarah Masters, met them as they walked in. "Hello, Mr. Moses. Excellent speech yesterday. I heard you had some interesting times after the meeting, too. Glad you are all safe! It sounds like it got frightening for a while. Is this Professor Darling? We heard you had a pretty scary situation in New York."

June smiled and responded, "Scary really doesn't cover it—terrifying was more like it. If it wasn't for Steven and the bodyguards, I don't know if I would have made it out of there! Thanks for asking."

"Let me show you the way to the President's office. Does either of you need anything? Coffee and juice are in the office, and we have a breakfast prepared if you would like?"

Steven responded as they walked to into the President's office, "I would love some sausage and eggs with some hash browns and toast if you don't mind. Can she get anything for you, June?"

"No, thank you. I just ate, but I would really like some orange juice and coffee. I will set up over here and begin recording the meetings if that's all right with you and President Stewart?"

"Did I hear my name?" President Stewart asked, smiling as he walked over to greet them. "Certainly, Professor Darling, if you want to record our meetings, it's just fine. We do ask that you withhold anything sensitive on security matters, and we ask you to not divulge them until later. We have nothing to hide in here, but much of it will be sensitive, and we want this recorded for future generations, God willing."

"Please call me June, and yes, I appreciate that and will not reveal anything sensitive until after all this is over. I am more interested in the actual history of this event than the details of the security issues."

"Thank you, June. Steven, I know it was a short night last night, but we have a full day today. After we grab a bite here, we're going to meet with our security people. It sounds like they have something that occurred last night. They shot down an aircraft invading our airspace, so they want to brief us on that and then discuss all the possibilities they believe could happen with this embargo. After that, we meet with Congress. We must discuss all the options they're going to be expected to deal with in relation to the social and economic realities of a severe economic downturn. So, enjoy your breakfast; you're going to earn this meal!"

The Security Council consisted of Major General Sutton, Border General Landrus, and Technology General Martinez. Major General Sutton was a native Texan who grew up in the Army and rose quickly through the ranks from his exploits in Iraq and Afghanistan as a multi-dimensional battlefield expert. He was one of the originators of combat coordination through AWACS and fast-attack tank warfare as well as warthog and helicopter support for the ground troops and their armored support advancing him into the inner corridors of the Pentagon, helping develop support tactics. His strategies were copied throughout the Pentagon. He was then moved to strategies and tactics used around the world.

The clouds were dark and thick over New York City as Secretary-General Polentas sat in her office. Sitting across from her was her NY City mercenary squad leaders headed up by Stazi Ramone and Shelton Liston. These two controlled the mobs of New York and handled all the insurrections. She looked at them through narrowed eyes.

"How can the Texas Christians still be causing us problems? You said you would have them taken care of months ago, and not only are they not taken care of, but they are also growing stronger and fighting in broad daylight. They're lynching your people, and the locals are sympathizing with them. I want them stopped, and I want them stopped now!"

Stazi was a thick Italian American who grew up on the streets promoting his Sicilian roots. He dreamed of becoming a big mafia boss but took a detour into the Union mob. He became a strong-arm guy, losing count of the number of broken arms and broken promises to his family he had made in his lifetime. He always could break a knee or issue a contract on a troublemaking leader to settle the dissension, but these Texas Christians and their leader, the Ranger, were different. Nothing scared them or intimidated them, as they were Christians and had a belief that could not be silenced by threats or intimidation.

He looked at Secretary-General Polentas and said, "Secretary-General, you don't understand. We have armies of unions and gangs who have been fighting them when we can find them, but they are like fighting smoke. You cannot corner them, and when you do, they fight like they have ten times their troops. We had them cornered two weeks ago in the warehouse district and had them beaten. Then the wind and rain came in, and they just escaped like ghosts. We killed a dozen of them, but there are thousands now, and we're having a hard time finding them."

She looked at them both and raged, "You listen, and you listen well. I want them dead. Do you hear me? I'm putting a bounty on each one of them of one hundred thousand dollars, and ten times that for their leader, the Texas Ranger. We're about to go to war with Texas, and the last thing we need to worry about is the security of New York—so if you two can't do this, then I will find people who can. Do you understand?"

Shelton Liston was quietly listening and felt the anger begin to well up in his belly. He was a large black man who grew up in the drug gangs in Harlem. He came from a single mother family with two sisters and grew up on the streets in the gangs who were his real family. He quickly became one of the leaders and was especially bright in the drug trades unifying the gangs into one mega-gang that controlled the entire city.

When his organization joined with the unions, they became one of the strongest forces in the city, virtually controlling the streets. Then came this Texas Ranger group who began fighting his gang and taking over entire neighborhoods using residents as snitches who pointed out and coordinated the attacks, knocking his shooting galleries out of the blocks and shutting down entire neighborhoods.

"Listen, Secretary-General Polentas; nobody wants these rangers out of the city more than we do. They are interfering with our entire operations. We will take you up on your bounties, and we will double the bounty on their leader. Just give us a little more time. We're getting closer and closer, but Stazi is right. These guys are hard to corner and fight like nothing we've seen before. They are well organized and understand how to fight and find weaknesses, as well as know the tunnels and passages of New York. Just give us a bit more time."

She looked at the two and wondered how she ever found two so incompetent leaders and answered, "That is just the problem: we don't have more time. I'm going to meet with the Security Council later today and propose they give me the power to declare war on Texas. They will give me that power, and then our entire focus is going to be to destroy and level their country and get it over quickly. The last thing I need is a street battle going on here while we're running people in and out of this city. I'll patch you into our security people who relate to the police and intelligence communities to find out who this guy is and his organization. We need to kill them, and we need to start yesterday. If we do not, we have a chance of having the sympathizers beginning to join them, and then our problems will multiply overnight. Our people will get in touch with you this afternoon and help you find these pests and put an end to them. Do you understand me? I want them dead, and especially this Texas Ranger!"

They looked at her and answered, "Yes, we understand, and we'll have his head on a platter within twenty-four hours. We have to go and meet our troops. We won't disappoint you this time. We'll find this instigator, and when we do, he will be dead. Thank you for your time."

She could hear the continual gunfire throughout the city. It had a dark sort of rhythm like a Caribbean drum beat that made your heart pound from the passion and coming violence off in the distance. The street battles were getting more pronounced as the gang wars became a way of life in the city. She didn't have time to be concerned with the problems in the city when she had a renegade country, causing her potential problems within her own coalition. Many of her political enemies were sympathetic with Texas and wanted her to take a softer tone than she was willing. She didn't want to begin a war with Texas, but to hold the world together, she knew she had to enforce the resolution to the full extent of her power and make sure it was over quickly. When this was done, the world would know there is truly one government, and she will be the one leader of this government.

Her personal assistant knocked on her door and brought in President Chambers, the UN military general, and Ambassador of Brazil, Ambassador Herrmoza. Herrmoza was a large chocolate-skinned man with a distinguished face and a well-trimmed black beard. His beard matched his dark eyes, which were narrow and cold from his wars against the drug cartels in the late teens. He was known as a great tactician and completely ruthless in his abilities to find a weakness in an enemy and then scorch the earth behind them. His treachery was only matched by his corruption. He was known to take bribes and drugs for the cartels' protection.

Secretary-General Polentas rose and welcomed the two men. "Gentlemen, you know the reason I called you here. We have passed the resolution, and now we need to explain to them what it means to them and the world. We need them to acquiesce to our demands and become full member of the UN. If they refuse, we need to force them to do this immediately, which means we must throw the full force of the world government behind our enforcement. I want this to be short and dramatic so no other nation will dare to show such resistance as we've seen from Texas. We're going to offer them a forty-five-day period to accept our demands, and if they don't, we have to be prepared to use anything at our disposal—both economically and militarily."

President Chambers spoke up, "Madame Secretary, I want this as much as you do, but don't you think we should fight this war diplomatically and strategically with sanctions, like we spoke of before, rather than militarily? And if I'm hearing you, it sounds as if you are not ruling out nuclear weapons. We can't—"

"President Chambers, you are in no position to say what we can or cannot do. You and your people are only able to survive thanks to the generosity of the UN and our ability to provide you assistance. You know what would happen to your country and your presidency if we were to cut off your power or funding to run all your utilities and industries. We have enough countries like yours that use the world's resources to provide for your ungrateful citizens like the ones fighting in the street. We need more countries that understand the power and might of this world government. Now, Ambassador Herrmoza, what do you have for me?"

Ambassador Herrmoza placed a minicomputer on her desk, which put a visual on the wall opposite them with a map of Texas and the surrounding area. "Madame Secretary, we have been working on this problem for over a year and have come up with a plan we believe will bring them to acceptance if we decide to go forward.

"We've been testing their defenses, and we believe we've found a number of weaknesses which we can exploit to gain access to their infrastructure. You will notice they have a series of oil wells throughout the Gulf, which are largely undefended. We can begin by knocking them out and then move in and destroy their refining capabilities here on the coast. We can have them completely unable to produce oil or export goods through their ports by sinking tankers and container ships in them, bringing them to the negotiating table. We predict this will get their attention and let them know we mean business. They'll be ready to accept our demands. We'll also be making a statement to any other countries who would be a world renegade."

Secretary Polentas responded, "You don't understand the Texans. If this plan would work and you would be able to close their ports and refining, what would stop them from fighting back and rebuilding their facilities? These Texans have backbones, and I doubt a few destroyed refineries and oil wells are going to make them quit. What would stop them from digging in and wanting to fight harder? I want them to understand we are not going to stop at destroying a few oil terminals. These Texans and the world must know and fear us. What else do you have?"

"I'm glad you asked, Madame Secretary, since we agree with you, and this is simply the first phase. When they turn down our offers for peace, we'll have already defeated their defenses and completely rule the air and space over their country, which means we will have access to their infrastructure and buildings throughout their industrial centers around Houston, Dallas, and their capital in Austin. Our first target will both be strategic and symbolic, which will be the Moses building and the surrounding buildings, destroying their financial and energy centers. At the same time, we will be leveling the Houston area as well as the Dallas metro complex and eliminating Austin, so there will be no communication or coordination throughout the country.

"Once we have neutralized the country, we'll send in our troops from Oklahoma, New Mexico, and from the Gulf. We expect the fighting will last no more than thirty days due to the lack of communication and the knowledge that their most important landmarks and centers have been destroyed, making a chaotic militia that will quickly be dispatched and neutralized, making them and their people demand a peace treaty."

President Chambers stood up, protesting, "This is insane, Madame Secretary! You are talking about killing perhaps hundreds of thousands if not millions of people and causing untold destruction that will take decades to replace. There are better ways to do this without all this death and destruction. You cannot be serious about doing this. I refuse to be a part of this!"

Polentas spoke through clenched teeth, "You have no choice, President Chambers. Without our help, you will be in a deeper recession without power or fuel within forty-five days. What do you think will happen to your political career once that is done?"

"I don't care about my career. You can't be making threats or wholesale killing of entire countries to make some sort of sick example so you can become the ruler of the world. My career is not worth my soul, and I won't go along with this. I am going to the Security Council to have this stopped."

Ambassador Herrmoza touched him on the back with a baton and hit a button, sending President Chambers' heart into a severe arrhythmia, forcing him to slump to the carpet as he stared in disbelief at the Secretary-General. She simply stared at him without blinking as he slipped into a black envelope of emptiness.

"I told you he wouldn't go along with this, but there is no way we could allow him to talk. Call the authorities and let them know this is an emergency. There will be no way for them to trace it; it's impossible to tell it from a heart attack. Call his Secret Service team."

"Before I do that, what is your plan if this doesn't force them to acceptance of the resolution?"

"Like you said, Madame Secretary, we are willing to use all options, both conventional and nuclear."

"That's what I thought. Now get that thing out of here while I call his Secret Service."

"I'll give you two minutes before I call them in."

Ambassador Herrmoza walked out the door and into the foyer past the Secret Service on his way to the elevators. As he entered the elevator, he slid the thin baton between the door and the wall and could hear it start to fall down the seventy-five floors, where it shattered into a thousand pieces.

TEXAS DECIDES

Steven Moses, President Stewart, June, and the rest of the room stared in disbelief at the monitor as they had over the last twenty-four hours while the United States Supreme Court Justice swore in Vice President Victoria Price as president. The entire world stood in absolute shock that President Chambers would die of a sudden heart attack in the UN. The timing and location seemed too convenient to be a heart attack, and the Grassy Knoll crowd had already begun posting conspiracies. Everything was moving so fast it was hard for them to keep up. Then the UN voted to enforce their sanctions with military force, putting them in a direct line toward World War with the United Nations.

"Well, there you have it, she's president," remarked President Stewart, breaking the silence. "I felt I could deal with Chambers, but I have no relationship at all with Price. I know she had a famous father who was a senator for years, but I've never met her. My guess is she will rubber-stamp everything coming out of the UN, which doesn't help us at all."

Steven looked over at him and around the room. "Do you really think he died naturally in Secretary Polentas' office?"

"We'll never know since whatever happened will be covered up by the authorities," President Stewart replied, "not to mention their friends in the media. I wouldn't put anything past them, but I have no proof, so it really doesn't matter. Unless they have some evidence, this could just be another conspiracy rumor. Our problem is, do we go to war with them or don't we? If we decide to go to war, we will be in for the biggest nightmare of our lives, and we have to consider the millions of Texans who will be hurt or killed."

Vice President Chavez spoke up, "Either way, it's going to be our biggest nightmare. If we agree to their resolution, we'll lose our economic future by having to give away so much of our revenues to the UN; and if we fight, we'll lose untold lives and suffer massive economic destruction to our industries. We have never set ourselves up to be a military power, so we have very little to fight them with. If they did kill President Chambers, we know what kind of people we're dealing with. That said, whatever you decide, I and the Texas people are behind you."

Steven spoke up, "What if we try to buy some time to develop some weapons? We have several of them on the drawing boards, and we have the platforms for weaponizing our aircraft as well as some of our armored vehicles. But we need some time to begin production. What if we agreed to their terms on a trial basis for six months?"

President Stewart responded, "Can we manage for six months in their control, and would the Congress agree? We would have to surrender to their terms without them finding out what we're doing. In the meantime, we would have to negotiate with them while we're developing our weapons programs before they discover them since we know at some point they will find out what we're doing. I would guess we could get somewhere between two days to four months before we would be found out, and then war would be declared. How long would it take before you could be producing weapons if we were to agree to their terms?"

"Well, Stew, we've been actually working on weapons for years and have several mock-ups of pretty conventional stuff like energized lasers and missiles, but we do have some ideas in the pipeline that we must have to fight such overwhelming forces. We will be outnumbered and outgunned by a hundred-to-one, not to mention all the advantages they have in satellite cover and having us surrounded. Even if we get the time and can work out some of the bugs in these recent technologies, it will take a miracle to keep them from our complete annihilation, and that is if they don't use nuclear weapons, which we have never developed.

"We need to take this to our Congress in a closed session to hammer out these choices," President Stewart replied thoughtfully. "But if it comes down to my decision, it will be to keep the embers of freedom burning. This is bigger than a few million Texans—this is about keeping the hope of mankind being able to choose his life as well as his government, which has only occurred a few times in history. Texas is the last stand of freedom, just like our forefathers at the Alamo. Remember them?"

As they walked into the hall, June's phone rang from a scrambled number. Answering it, she heard the familiar voice of the Texas Ranger. "Hey, Professor, that was a pretty close call we had when you came to visit. I've been holed up and on the run, but it looks like we finally shook them, although they seem to be more aggressively hunting us. There are all sorts of rumors floating around about President Chambers' death and if it was an assassination. Most think they had some sort of undetectable drug to stop the heart. Nobody is sure how they did it, but he died in Polentas' office, which is just too convenient. What are you hearing?"

Jane came back, "Nobody here has any idea of what happened other than what is being reported. It sounds suspicious that he would have a heart attack in the UN Secretary General's office at this time. Either he was under unbelievable stress, or someone had a hand in it. We'll never know. It's so good to hear your voice. How did you get out of there?"

"It was pretty lucky, but we have a lot of ex-military, and they always have contingency plans. This was one of those. Let's just say we were able to give more than we took and left them in bad shape. That brought out their big guns, and they all but leveled our church and a few other meeting houses. It's become open season for Christians. That's okay—the church always grows the fastest during the harshest persecution. I just wanted to let you know we're well; we have some big things coming up, our numbers are growing, and we're really making headway against their forces. Take care, and I'll be in touch."

"Hey, I wanted to tell you what I found in your data?"

"Not right now. I will call you next week when you have a chance to talk. See ya. I have to go!"

Ranger closed his phone just as his detection sensors started beeping. He had been triangulated again, and the hovers were closing in. The bullets and lasers began lighting up the area as a large force of union gangs, and UN support started firing from airborne platforms. His men began firing back, and the perimeter forces began taking on the hovers. The new anti-air handhelds were a godsend as they began dropping a couple and holding off the ones closing in. He heard the ground vehicle sirens coming in, which were likely the police coming to quash his fellow rebels.

His men and he began to counterattack to allow the bulk of his forces to escape into the maze of buildings, tunnels, and sewers that made up Brooklyn. That's when he saw the largest hover he had ever seen come out of nowhere. It came banking out of the south river, circling their positions, firing from every angle. It was a full city block large and had at least fifty lasers shooting in all directions using computer identification and targeting. In addition to the firepower, it had some type of digital panels that stopped his teams' fixed-platform lasers and redirected the beams back at the platforms, blowing them to pieces. He watched as his men and weapons fell ten stories to their deaths. His heart fell the ten stories with them, knowing his strategy was going to make over fifty families fatherless.

Although the size and mass of this machine were immense, it had speed and agility to move faster than any hover he had seen while having the ability to maneuver between buildings to get near street level. It was targeting all his men in perimeter positions, and their anti-air weapons had no effect on this craft as it killed them in microseconds. This was when he gave the order to disengage and fall back to a safer location. He watched as his men were slaughtered or captured while he and his main group were able to hide under the overpasses and maze of tunnels to escape this latest weapon of destruction.

His men returned to their most secure hideout below Queens and assessed the damages. His officers reported to him that they suffered seventy-eight killed and dozens wounded and captured, although they wouldn't be able to assess until they had a chance to regroup. They all knew the captured would be given a quick trial and either hanged or shipped to the work camps in upstate or Montana and the Dakotas.

The Republic of Texas

As they talked and he reassessed their situation, he knew the tide had turned, and his group's days were numbered.

Ranger spoke to the hundreds assembled. "Ladies and gentlemen, you all know what the situation is: we are all outlaws in our own city. We have become outlaws by defending our city from the gangs and unions who are supported by the One World Government of the UN. We have been fighting for our freedom, and only by the grace of God have we survived this long. We lost some good men today who have fought with us, side by side. We lost Peter Summers and Josh Carpenter, who have been fighting with us since this movement began. We lost many friends who are with Jesus tonight, and we are all hurting for them, but they are in glory.

"I am releasing everybody here from their pledges to fight this battle against these impossible odds. You need to go now and raise your families and live long, happy lives rather than get killed fighting against something we can't overcome. We've made a statement, and they're only after me. So, it's time for me to do the right thing and turn myself in before we're all wiped out. I'm disbanding our army so you can all be safe again."

David Thomas, a twenty-two-year-old ex-punk rocker, walked forward and spoke loudly, "Who are you to tell us when and where we can lay down our lives for freedom? What good is living a long and happy life if you live that life under the fear of a government that can take your life from you whenever they want? If they have you, it won't stop them from doing what they did tonight. They'll only hunt us down harder. I, for one, will fight with you or someone else who will take your place to the death with me and my wife. I would rather die fighting to breathe the cool breath of freedom than die of old age breathing the stench and acrid smell of oppressive government slavery. Just like Nathan Hale said in our revolution hundreds of years ago, 'I regret that I have but one life to give for my country.' Or, as Patrick Henry put it, 'Give me liberty or give me death.'

"I remember when I was a young boy, we had a free country, but we gave it away. We let the government grow and intrude in our lives more and more, thanks to apathy and selfishness. We have one chance to get that country back, and only by the mercy of Jesus Christ our Lord and Savior will we be able to do that. As for me, my wife, and my family, we will give our dying breaths to return that liberty to this once great country—America. Who is with me?"

In the back of the room, someone started singing; then the entire room began to sing that chorus, "Ohhhhh, say can you see, by the dawn's early light…"

Steven, June, and President Stewart entered the Senate chambers, which were filled to standing room only. President Stewart went straight to the podium. "Thank you, everybody, for coming. You know the gravity of this meeting, and I need to remind you this is the highest security for everything that is going to be discussed today. Only the highest security clearances are to be attending today, and anybody without those security clearances must leave now."

Several aides and assistants shuffled out of the auditorium, leaving only senators, congressmen, and military who needed to be part of the decision-making process.

"Ladies and gentlemen, we have one of the most difficult decisions we've ever had to make. I don't have to remind you; you cannot speak of anything we are going to be discussing today. You should consider that as of this minute, we are in a state of war, and anything you say outside of the proper channels could not only compromise our plans but cost thousands of lives.

"You are all aware that we have been given an ultimatum to sign Resolution 2033–311 or face the consequences of force, which would certainly mean a sea blockade and, highly likely, military action. We should expect the worst since we all know they need to make an example of any independent country that is willing to stand against the United Nations and its governing authority. They will show what can happen to countries no matter how big, and they have warned us there would be mass casualties and destruction with no mercy being shown.

"We all remember the brutal atrocities that were shown by the UN forces in the uprisings in India, Brazil, and Spain. You can imagine what they are capable of with a country like Texas. They need to make an example of what can happen if you cross the UN Security Council. This may or may not include nuclear weapons if they see the need.

"The worst part is we have not completed our weapon-making capabilities, so we are essentially defenseless minus a few hovercraft and jets with light laser capabilities. We have some old missiles from when we were a state that were left to us, but without any stealth technologies or reflective digital, they would be lucky to make it out of their silos. We do have advanced weapons in the design and testing stages, but to be turned into usable weapons, we need time to develop them.

"Everybody understands the UN and the world have all of the wartime weapons they're using and developing constantly in their peace-keeping activities. This means they have and know how to effectively use their military, which would overwhelm us before we can get our weapons developed or deployed. So, what we need to do is one of two things: either we comply with their resolution, or we appear to comply while we are buying time. Every one of you must understand what this means if we are exposed, and they decide to punish us for it. We're looking at a real possibility of being completely leveled if we go to war or economically destroyed if we agree. If we buy some time and fail to do it, we will be at war within twenty-four hours, and you all understand what that would mean. Does anybody have any questions?"

Major General Thompson spoke up. "I am in complete agreement that we need to buy whatever time we can, if possible. But does everyone here believe these congressmen or Texans are going to accept giving up their freedom and sovereignty to as untrustworthy an institution as the UN? They are all ready to fight, as you see every night on the net streams. How do you think they will react if we accept the proposals and have to keep the actual reasons secret? The Texas National Guard is not going to want to begin fighting Texans when they are ready to fight the Blue Helmets."

"That's a good point, General Thompson, and right now, we're not sure how we're going to present this to the people of Texas," President Stewart responded. "Our initial thought is that we should promote the idea that we are attempting to protect them from the death and destruction of war. We must explain we would lose most of our manufacturing facilities, including the oil terminals and refineries, as well as the auto and surrounding industries in the first two weeks because they are completely defenseless. There would be mass casualties inside those facilities and surrounding communities because of the fires and destruction, as well as collateral damage and casualties. We would have to make that clear to our fellow Texans, yet not give any indication we are developing our fighting capabilities behind the scenes."

Senator Stanson from Houston spoke up, "Well, I, for one, do not like this program for one second, but if General Thompson confirms what President Stewart has to say, then my county will go along with the program as long as we have an understanding there will be payback in short order. Now a couple of things I would like to suggest that occurred to me while this discussion was going on. First, we can still buy some time before the UN regulators come in to shut down all our so-called polluting industries in Houston and elsewhere. What if we offer to buy our sovereignty for a sum like what we paid the United States?

"At the drop-dead date, we could offer a buyout to get us a few months' time before they come in and not only hurt our manufacturing but also begin looking over our scientists' shoulders as they continue to develop these programs. This would buy us some time with the UN and would give us time with our citizens who are ready to start World War III.

"Let's also not forget the United States needs our petroleum products as well as electrical generation. If we shut down, they will be crippled worse than we will. There are a few levers that we can pull to make them think twice about attacking us and destroying our energy production. They would be 'cutting off their nose to spite their face.'

"They need to understand that if they were to drop a nuclear weapon, they would suffer as much as us from the destruction of our energy generation. They could only survive a few months without our power plants, and although we would suffer the deaths immediately, they would suffer as many if not more deaths from the lack of power and from the mass anarchy that would come from our destruction."

Rattler was flying the converted F-23 over the Gulf, taking it through its paces, enjoying the feel of an aircraft that possessed precision and power. He had flown Navy fighters, which were supposed to be identical, but these had far more updated technology and power than anything he had ever flown before. The weaponry was far advanced of anything in the arsenals of any of the air forces around the world since Texas Instruments supplied most of the world's military. He was happy to move back to fighters from the hover jets he had been flying. The power and maneuverability of the fighter gave him a feeling of invincibility he hadn't felt in many years. These fighters had far faster acceleration and more maneuverability than anything he had flown before. The computer-assisted flying reacted as fast as you could touch the joystick.

Commander Jackson spoke over the headset, "Rattler, give the ramjet a try. You need to get used to the speed of this aircraft. Hit the ramjet booster, and you will accelerate to Mach 7 for ten minutes. This will allow you to escape any aircraft or attack an enemy before he has any chance to detect you on laser."

"Roger that, Commander Jackson. Scanning the horizons and satellites; Horizons scanned. Going ramjet in five, four, three, two, one, fire." He hit the ramjet trigger and heard the air intakes surge in power as the aircraft began to shudder. He was immediately thrown into the back of his seat as his helmet molded into his headrest. He could feel the G-suit inflate while he pushed hard on his abdomen, feeling the blood begin to leave his head and his eyeballs sink into their sockets. His jet immediately shot him up to ninety thousand feet and was flying at nearly four thousand miles per hour in ninety seconds, yet he kept complete control of his aircraft.

The feeling was more exhilarating than he had ever experienced, knowing there was nothing that could come close to staying with him other than the shuttle and rockets. Yet very few air-to-air or surface-to-air aircraft could begin to catch him if they were able to detect his signature. The aircraft diversion software protection would deflect any laser weaponry and have him out of range in seconds. After the ten-minute burn, the ramjet stopped, and he switched back to jet power, doing a few loops, rolls, and spins to let off the excitement while testing the maneuverability of the aircraft. *This will be a formidable weapon in the war against the UN*, he thought.

Senator Stanson spoke up, "I don't know why we're dancing around when we know this is going to be a war sooner or later, and most likely sooner. I say we need to tell them to take their resolution and stuff it where the sun don't shine. Sure, they're going to blockade us and most likely attack us; but, if we can hold them off for two months and starve the world of refined petroleum and power, they will be begging for the UN to settle this. We all know this is going to end at the same place, so why not just get it over and be done with it? I can tell you, my constituents in Houston are ready and willing to fight and then deal with the consequences. We've had enough of the UN bullying us and every other country around like they own us."

A loud cheer swept across the chambers as the mood in the hall began to turn.

Senator Davis followed up, "I agree with Senator Stanson. We may not be ready, and we will be in better shape in a couple of months; but why should we cower to their demands? Did our forefathers negotiate with Santa Ana at the Alamo? No, they fought like Texans and died with their boots on. I say we push as hard as we can to get our weapons up and turn off the power to the US to let them know what they can expect. We are not going to bow down to their demands. I want them to know there are still Texans who are willing to die with their boots on and to take that final breath of freedom. They need to know that nobody messes with Texas, and that goes double for the United Nations! Remember the Alamo, Texans!"

Another loud cheer arose with shouts of "Remember the Alamo" as the members of the chamber began to become excited.

President Stewart looked over at Steven and asked him to the podium. "My fellow Texans, y'all know Steven Moses, and we can see that many of you are serious about going to war. Let him speak to you about the ability to cut off the power to the United States and what that would potentially mean."

Steven walked forward. "Well, as y'all know, this has never been attempted, let alone accomplished, but we have been studying it and sending test models through the grid over the last six months. What we have found is there are several weak points in the grid in both the Midwest outside Chicago and Columbus as well as Philadelphia, Newark, DC, and New York, which we call junction breakers, which could cripple the entire network.

"What our engineers have found is that if we were to trigger these weakened transmitters and cause them to fail, they would not know we had turned off the power; and they would be blacked out for anywhere from twenty-four to seventy-two hours, perhaps up to a week in certain areas. It would look exactly like a grid malfunction that just tripped substations like dominoes. When they did get back on line, they would find we were not generating, but it would look like we had a back-surge knocking out our transmission lines and stations. Now, they may eventually figure it out, but it would give us a couple of weeks while the

United States was completely dark in many of the populated areas. Any questions?"

Senator Stanson stood up. "Mr. Moses, does this have a chance of permanently destroying their electrical grid, or would it simply be temporary? And could you aim this at certain cities like New York and Washington, DC?"

"No, it wouldn't physically damage anything other than a few transfer stations, which would be repaired, and no, we cannot aim it. Once you trip the switch, it will simply spread across the trunk lines and transformers like a spiderweb blacking out state by state with no real way of stopping it. Once the web starts building, there is no way of knowing how or where it would go or what cities would be blacked out.

"Now, understand: this is all theory since we haven't actually done it on a massive scale like this, but you will remember the brownouts these cities had two months ago from failing substations. We're confident we can make this happen. They will then route power down from Canada and up from Mexico, which means they'll be on limited power for the duration, blacking out cities they decide can be blacked out to save energy."

The debates went on well into the evening, offering resolution after resolution until the final ballots were cast and President Stewart stepped to the podium. "Ladies and gentlemen, the resolution is passed, and we have decided to reject United Nations Resolution 2033–311 and are now considered in a state of world war. God help us all, and may God watch over Texas."

After the vote, June and Steven took off in the Black Stallion and flew south into the Gulf. He suggested they fly out one last time since the Gulf will be a no-fly zone as soon as the UN finds out that the resolution agreement was voted down, and they would soon be making military blockades. June enjoyed watching the sun melt into the blue and violet curved horizon fading behind them. It didn't feel like they were at war, although she could feel a knot in her stomach saying otherwise. This was an emotional day sitting as a witness to one of the most historic events in Texas history. She was mind-scribing on her computer as she watched all the shipping, hover traffic, and fishing boats working their nets for one of the last times in who knows how long.

She marveled at all the seemingly chaotic movement, yet it was the dance of commerce as everybody pursued their own dreams, which only they knew what those were and where they were hoping to go. She looked over at Steven and wondered what he was thinking. He carried so much of the world on his shoulders and had to know he could lose everything in a matter of days.

She put down her mind-scriber and asked, "Are you afraid of this war?"

He looked over at her and simply smiled. "No, what can they take from me? I have everything I want now. I have my faith, my health and family, and I have found you. I have been blessed more than any man deserves. If it goes away, I have lived a life I only dreamed of as a child. As long as you will never leave my side, I have all I want."

She just smiled as a tear moistened her cheek, and she laid her head on his shoulder the remainder of the flight, knowing she too had everything she ever wanted. Soon she saw the flight beacon of Platform 276 appear on the horizon. She could see the platform covered with hover jets and boats tied up to the docks all around the platform. Steven fluttered to a hover and settled down, landing in the middle of the last parking space on the deck. They got out, smelling the sweet salty breeze of the Florida Keys blowing across their faces as they walked to the entrance.

They took the elevator down into the sea, and as they entered the Submariner Restaurant, they were met by Terrance Jasmine with his wide smile and wider blue tuxedo, filling the entry with his laugh. "My favorite customers delighting me with your company again. What brings Steven and June Darling to my ocean floor paradise? I couldn't be happier to have such a lovely couple dining with me tonight."

"We just wanted to get down here one more time before who-knows-what happens. Things just seem to be spinning out of control up on top, and we wanted to get away from it all for an evening together and escape into the sea."

"Well, that sounds ominous, but you are in my place now, and there are seventy-five feet of sea, barracudas, and sharks between you and the real world. Come, please, let me seat you at the best table we have, and we will get you started with some drinks, appetizers, and entertainment."

Terrance led them to the center table by the windows. They sat and were served pineapple drinks in a coconut shell. He started the music, which began the water show. The dolphins swam across the stage and did their choreography, swimming in and out of the Acropolis columns and statues, followed by schools of multicolored fish being herded by another pod of dolphins. The divers swam through their dance routines moving with the music that flooded the room, and finally, two divers swam from opposite sides of the stage, one man in a tuxedo diving suit and the girl wearing a bride's veil, unrolling a sign that read, "Will you marry me, June Darling?"

June looked over at Steven, who was on his knees, holding a small black box and the largest diamond ring she had ever seen. Under the diamond was a triangular-shaped ruby set in a white gold setting.

"The diamond represents the sunlight you are in my life, and the ruby is the scar in my heart from Sandy's death. One represents my broken past and the other our bright future together."

Her eyes filled with tears as she covered her face. He looked up into her eyes and said, "June, you know I love you, and I know you love me. I want to spend the rest of my life with you, however long that will be. Will you please be my wife?"

June was in shock as the tears began to flow out of her eyes. She reached out to hug and kiss him while she sobbed, "Yes." He slipped the ring on her finger, which was lit by a spotlight somewhere in the ceiling. The setting had two tiny golden dolphins swimming around the ring with a large derrick-shaped diamond in the middle, sitting above the triangular ruby.

Just then, the lights lowered, and multicolored bubbles began falling from the ceiling with a multicolored laser display lighting the underwater columns and divers as the restaurant applauded. Terrance came walking out, grinning from ear to ear with both of their parents. "He got you, *ma cherie*! Congratulations to you both, although I don't know what you see in this man. You could have done a lot better, *ma cherie*!"

June looked weakly as her tears flowed freely. "Mom? Daddy?"

"June Bug, we are so happy for you. He called us last week and asked for your hand in marriage, and I said only if I can marry you two! Your mother and I had a pretty good idea you would say 'yes,' so we agreed to come out here. What a place! I ain't crazy about being on the bottom of the ocean in a glass bubble, but this is beyond beautiful."

Her mother was dressed in pink chiffon that made her look like an underwater fairy with the light glittering off the sparkles. Her eyes were filled with tears as she came over to hug her daughter. "This is so beautiful, and you make such a handsome couple. I know you will both be happy. Welcome to the family, Steven. We've been waiting for you." That made them all laugh.

William and Carol Moses stepped forward and congratulated Steven and June and hugged them all.

William Moses looked at June. "We couldn't be happier for you to be his wife. You have no idea how hurt he was when he lost Sandy. It was as if he had his arm cut off, and we watched as he retreated into his work and ignored his personal life. You have changed all of that, and we couldn't be prouder of him or happier for you two."

Tears rolled down June's cheeks as she hugged them both.

"I am stunned, Terrance. How did you two pull this off?"

"Ahhh, *ma cherie*, he called last week, and we put it all together for him. For you, we provide anything. Now be prepared for the best crab stuffed mahi-mahi you have ever had. I hope you brought your appetite, *cherie*. You are going to need it!"

"Of course, I did! Today was the longest day of my life, and now it is the happiest; but yes, I am starved. Thank you, Steven. I love you so much it hurts! Can we get married right away? I don't believe this is happening."

The restaurant began applauding and wishing them a happy future together as the party was just beginning.

NEW YORK CHRISTIAN CHURCH

Ranger rose to give his speech in a deserted school auditorium in front of over two thousand cheering fans and parishioners. "As you all have heard, last week Texas rejected UN Resolution 2033–311, and now they're deciding what actions they're going to take. You all need to pray for our brothers and sisters in Texas for their protection and safety: the winds of World War III are surely about to rain down on them. I also shouldn't have to tell you; we're all in even more danger than we've ever been before.

"We have no way of knowing what this means for us in New York City, but we should be prepared for martial law as well as tightened security throughout the city, if that's possible. We're all going to have to take some extra precautions so we're not seen or captured in the city sweeps coming our way. We won't be having any more of these large rallies. We'll need to have our assemblies on the secure net and use all your masking software to confuse the spyware and spiders. From this point on, we all need to be considered even higher priority targets than we've been in the past.

"Folks, how did we get here? For all of you Americans and New Yorkers who grew up here, you must ask yourselves, how did this tyranny ever come to be? How in America does a group that simply wants to enjoy freedom become Public Enemy Number One of the United States, let alone the world? And how does one of our fellow states that seceded become the enemy of the entire world simply for wanting to hold onto its sovereignty? It's simple how this happened: good people stopped paying attention and caring about their country, and their country vanished. It has now been taken over by the very people whom we considered our enemies ten years ago. Little by little, they took more and more—until we became their subjects.

"Brothers and sisters, you have to remember who you are. You are proud, God-fearing Americans who do not need the government to make your every decision and provide your every need. You are the people who conquered the oceans, crossed the prairies and those western mountains in wagons. You are the people who fought off the most powerful tyrannies around the world numerous times; and now we need to be those people once more. They are here in New York and throughout the country—Americans who are all starving for the truth and looking for leadership. We need to reach out to those people and recruit them into our ranks. We need to cause the tyrants as much problem as we can while their focus is on defeating Texas. We need to distract their focus so the Texans can have a chance of winning.

"Even though there will be a crackdown on our movements, it's doubtful they will be able to fight the war and have enough men to find us with our underground routes. We still can use our subway avoidance methods for overcoming their detection monitors. The past five years have taught us ways to get in, and out of places nobody in the city even knows about, or where these tunnels go, or our hidden entries.

"We owe it to our Texan brothers and sisters to make things as difficult as we can for the United Nations to fight this war. You all know that if you're caught, you're likely going to be sentenced to imprisonment or hanging. We need to have the heart and courage to maintain a war in the belly of the beast. Many of you will not make it out of this war, but you will have given everything you have to the cause of freedom. The advantage we have is we know these people better than they know themselves. This is the last stand for freedom, or we will all die trying."

A chant started across the crowd: "Freedom, Freedom, Freedom or death! Freedom, Freedom, Freedom, or death! …"

"Yes, my brothers and sisters, this is our fight for freedom. We have been oppressed and taken advantage of for far too long. We can go back to the times when they had fair and free elections—when people's votes were counted. We can go back to self-rule and bring our republic back to be represented by the people and where the people rule."

Just then, the entire outside of the building lit up like a movie set. They could hear shooting begin on the roof. Spotlights were shining from police hovers as well as the street spots being directed from the tops of the skyscrapers lighting the entire area like it was the middle of day.

"Battle stations, everybody! Women and children hit the escape routes and get moving. We will give you a twenty-minute head start and be right behind. Meet at the designated meeting locations for your teams. Prayer warrior teams, pray for our victory!"

The gunbattle was in full combat as Ranger moved outside. They were surrounded by UN police and gangs as well as some of the special union forces. The air was covered with hovers darting in and out of the New York canyons. An anti-air laser opened fire on one coming at them, and you could see the digital deflection shield was lit up like a fireworks display. Suddenly it lit up deep red and exploded into a giant ball of flames crashing into a warehouse. They knew they were outnumbered and outgunned. They fought with a ferocious tenacity, trying to give the women and children time to escape down through the maze of tunnels. The prayer warriors continued praying for a miracle to allow their escape and to allow a victory.

Then they heard the now-familiar screech coming from up the East River that froze the spine of every man on the ground. A Hover Fortress came roaring over the battlefield, firing lasers in every direction, killing his men by the dozens. The battle turned to chaos as they retreated toward the school side entrance, which was cut off by the block-sized killing machine. It was impossible for them to cross as the entire parking lot was lit by spotlights being shown from the tops of tall buildings on either side. The loudspeakers were demanding their surrender and to put down their weapons or face certain death. His entire force was pinned down behind abandoned cars and trucks and hidden under the school walkways as the police and gangs were fighting their way toward them. It was only a matter of time before they were captured or killed.

Susan Bennett was leading the women and children through the tunnels as quickly as she could. The leaders had night vision headlamps. She knew these underground mazes as well as anybody in New York. She grew up with her brothers playing and transporting Bibles through this network, which allowed her travel below ground faster than most New Yorkers could above. Just as they turned the corner that linked into the subway rendezvous, the entire tunnel lit up from rows of overhead lights as they looked and saw around fifty police officers waiting for them in an ambush. They looked behind, and there was another group of gang members now blocking their exit, carrying portable spotlights, turning the dark into the brightest day with nowhere to hide.

One of the police officers spoke through a megaphone and said, "Ladies, don't move or try to escape. We won't hurt you, but you must surrender and come out of those tunnels. Now come over here—nice and slow! If you have weapons, drop them, and surrender peacefully. You owe it to your children; we won't harm them or you if you cooperate."

The Ranger huddled together with his captains and discussed whether to surrender or fight it out and try to break through when something caught his eye across the river and started seeing white explosions and buildings going black. It quickly moved their direction as they heard what sounded like shotguns going off and large flashes followed by darkened blocks, when suddenly a flash lit up the transformer across the street in a spark-cascading explosion. All the lights around them went dark, including the spotlights covering their escape. There appeared to be mass confusion as this happened, and they could hear the police yelling for instructions as their radios and computers went dark. That's when he yelled to make a break for the school building. They ran for all they were worth, getting inside the school and down through the tunnels and into the blackened city.

Susan Bennett was praying for their group as the police portable spotlights went black, giving her a chance to direct everyone to take the side tunnel leading to their designated rendezvous. She heard the confusion of the police behind her as they replaced the false brick covering of their escape tunnel and headed to the emergency meeting site while praying for the men's safety. She had no idea why the lights went out, but it was a miraculous answer to her prayers.

President Stewart, Steven, June, Vice President Sanchez, and Sam Satterwhite, Texas Secretary of Energy, watched the giant wall monitor of the US grid as the rolling blackout moved across the country until the entire screen was dark. After it finished like an intricate rolling domino collapse, they looked at each other, knowing that this was going to cause untold pain and suffering in their old country. They all knew this had to be done to buy some time before the military attacks began. If they waited, the attacks would likely be coming in the morning. Who knows, they may come anyway, although it was highly likely they shut down the United Nation's communication for the short term. They would have little time to organize an attack on Texas while trying to figure out how to stop the people from rioting because of no electricity.

Sam looked at the screen in amazement and then turned to the group. "Well, it looks like the surge torpedo worked. We had our questions as to whether this would cause isolated blackouts with some brownouts rather than a rolling blackout. There is no way for them to trace it since when they isolate it, they will find a substation outside Cleveland is what tripped this event. With the age of the grid, a blown transformer will be found to be the culprit. They may have their usual suspicions, but after they run their tests and models, it will always point to Cleveland rather than Texas. That is some amazing technology that could send a surge torpedo through the power lines and begin tripping breakers all along the lines. The final piece of this technology is that it destroyed our power bridges across the border, so it will take weeks to repair them on our side to potentially bring us back on the line. We can delay repairs for up to eight weeks due to our lack of adaptability to the United States technology before they know we are dragging our feet, but they will be expecting that.

"Right now, any building that has emergency power or diesel backup is trying to get on the line and restore as much power as they can. The governments, including the UN and US, are trying to reroute to Canada and Mexico, although some of those may have been damaged in the blackout. This is going to take three to five days and perhaps a few more before they are back to functioning on a limited basis. Once they begin to recover, they will have to decide how to ration the power, which means they are going to have to decide which are the most vital cities and which are not. The rest of the cities will be dark and will have critical food and fuel problems complicating their recovery. Right now, the UN is functioning at around ten to twenty percent and has nobody to communicate to or have any idea of what is left with power. For the next forty-eight to seventy-two hours, they will be assessing the damage, as will we."

Steven walked to the front of the room, "Folks, we have just caused our old friends to become basically a third-world country in a matter of minutes. They may as well be in the middle of Brazil because they have no power, water, or transportation. The difference is, even though they've had hard times over the last few years, they have never experienced life with limited electrical power, and we must return it as soon as we can. We now are the most powerful and advanced country on earth since we have unlimited power and only a week or two before this war will begin in earnest. This also will give them an idea of what to expect if they are to destroy our generating capacity. They will suffer along with us.

"We have a short window of opportunity to prepare for battle. With the rejection of our stalling tactics from the Texas Congress, we must make every minute count and begin to set up defenses and design weapons. Everything must be put on a rush schedule and become usable yesterday. This is our chance to produce as much advanced weaponry as we can, and my companies will work around the clock to make sure this happens."

President Stewart looked around the room. "This was an utterly amazing event. How your engineers made this happen is beyond me, and a miracle it took out the entire US. I understand your feelings for them,

Steven, but they declared war on us, not the other way around; and they deserve whatever punishment they receive. They won't be worrying about Texas when they and the United Nations begin destroying our industries and cities or wiping out oil platforms. Texans will potentially be dying, and that is what I care about, not whether a city is lit up or a gas station is working. They should have considered that possibility when they allowed the UN to use them. We now have an upper hand for a couple of weeks, and it's time for our people to make the most of it."

Ranger and his forty best fighters had been driving all night to get to the Rome, NY, Re-education Camp that held twenty-five thousand political prisoners. With the power out and the mass confusion in the streets, they believed this would be the ideal time to help some of their friends and allies escape and swell his ranks. They pulled up on the south side of the camp with the lake on the opposite side. They could see that it was still lit up under emergency power and could hear the generator rumbling, but large areas were darkened without good lighting. That's where they were heading.

The only good part of being on the run is that they always had fuel in storage depots. The underground network would provide enough for missions like this. Most city dwellers had given up on owning cars due to the lack of gas, but his network was filled with underground survivalists who had stockpiles of staples like fuel. They parked the cars five hundred yards from camp while Ranger addressed the group. "Men, you all know this is going to be a high-risk mission. You may be killed or captured, and then you will be spending ten years inside this prison. You also know this is our opportunity to grow our army with thousands of our experienced Christian warriors back from the camp. These men and women were some of our best-trained fighters and technicians, and we have a real chance to get them back, so here is how we are going to get inside.

"I want the technicians and scouts to take out the auxiliary generator in the middle of the compound, which should be guarded. I need you to knock it out and make the prison yard dark. Tommy, you know how to get your guys over the fences without being detected—you are the key to this. Once you blackout the grounds, we will cut through the fences while you're getting into the cell blocks and opening the doors. We will be thirty seconds behind you once the lights go out and you take care of the tower guards. When the prisoners begin filling the camp, the guards should give up and worry more about getting home rather than being killed by their prisoners. We'll have the advantage of surprise – there's no way anybody is expecting this. Let's say a prayer and get going. You guys ready?"

Tommy Davis led a group of five men to the darkest section of fence and took off his backpack. As a one-time jewel thief who had broken into the tightest museums in the world, this was child's play. Inside the pack was a digitally synchronizing ladder and paralyzing Kevlar razor wire cover. It was in a spring-loaded catapult that shot it over the razor wire and digitally censored the fence detection and electrification. Once his ladder contacted the sensors, it eliminated their signal and allowed the men to climb up and over the fence. Once they got inside, they made it to the generator shack, where they shot the men with laser stun guns while their engineers shut down and disabled the generator, making the prison completely dark while opening the magnetic door locks to the cell blocks as a safety feature. As they headed for the prisoner barracks, they could see the rest of the teams coming through the fence, which is when the shooting started from the guard towers.

Ranger's men systematically returned fire and had the upper hand of not only having the advantage of surprise, but they all had night lenses while the guards were searching for theirs, making them easy targets. The rest of the guards had no night lenses and began surrendering immediately once they realized the attackers could see while they were blind men. The barracks began emptying as the remaining guards started running toward the lake and into the surrounding woods. His men fired a

The Republic of Texas

few shots in their direction, but they knew they wouldn't be back; and they entered the prison to free the prisoners.

When they turned a corner, they saw they were in what looked like an infirmary, except for all the people on the beds were dead. Both men and women were on gurneys with tubes coming out of their arms, but there was no movement. As they checked them, they found them warm with no pulse. Just then, prisoners came around the corner, and they stopped to look at the room full of dead bodies as the horror hit their faces.

They all walked through the room to the double doors out the back, which led to a large morgue and crematorium oven that had multiple doors to dispose of the bodies. It looked as if they could burn hundreds of bodies at any given time.

One of the prisoners spoke up, "Hi, my name is Tom Shelton. This is the Adirondack Death Camp. There are fewer than a thousand of us left. We make furniture as long as we can provide free labor, but once we are unable to provide that, thanks to the starvation rations, we join these people and become ashes for the cornfields. They dispose of over five thousand of us per month, mostly political prisoners."

Ranger just shook his head. "My name is Ranger, and I'm their number one political dissident. There are supposed to be more than twenty-five thousand prisoners here. How long have you been here, and how long has this been going on?"

"I've been here almost a year, which is longer than most last, especially during the winter when they turn the heat off in the barracks. This has been going on longer than I've been here. We've heard rumors there are around twenty or thirty of these camps spread across America."

"Is this everybody, and are there women's barracks?"

"No, there's only one women's cell block. They're brought here immediately since they're considered expendable unless they're attractive to temporarily become the guards' mistresses, or they are exceptional accountants or another needed skill, but they really don't want much of this accounted for, so those positions are scarce. I believe there may be five or ten still here on the north end of the camp. Do you want me to show you where it is?"

"Sure, take some of my men and bring them out. We'll be leaving in ten minutes. Take plenty of video of this infirmary, boys. We need this news to get out to the United States and the world."

The horror of this camp took Ranger back to his reading about the death camps in Germany and Russia, but he never imagined he would ever see one in America. He had a rage that went to his core, knowing his brothers and sisters were being murdered by the tens of thousands for the crime of being Christians and fighting for freedom. This was a crime against humanity, yet there was nobody to enforce it. A feeling of helplessness began at the base of his spine, making him want to vomit until the rage crept back in.

They could see the lights of the bus convoy coming in the distance as they pointed the prisoners to where the hole in the fence was and to head over to the now lit trucks in which they had just arrived. Ranger's men guarded the escape to make sure no guards decided to be heroes and begin shooting at his new recruits, although after seeing what he just saw, he wasn't sure if he wouldn't start shooting first.

Madame Secretary Polentas addressed the assembled Security Council. "Ladies and gentlemen, thank you for making the effort of coming to this security meeting to address Texas' rejection of UN Security Measure 2033-311. Even though we are experiencing extreme power blackouts in many regions of the United States, we have been assured by the United States government that they will have a majority of New York City back to full power within forty-eight to seventy-two hours. We have enough diesel fuel to provide emergency power until then. As the local citizens continue to conform to emergency protocols, the UN compound will soon be back on public power.

The Republic of Texas

"As for the matter at hand, we must decide what options we have to convince Texas they need to join the world community. Until we have our power back on the line, we recommend we simply declare and enforce a sea and land embargo of all goods going in and coming out of Texas. This is manageable and would allow us to negotiate with Texas to provide them an opportunity to return to the negotiating table and accept UN 2033–311. A blockade would show we are doing everything we can to negotiate while projecting strength under these circumstances. The world needs to understand Texas is being unreasonable while we are reaching out to avoid military action. The floor is now open for discussion. Mr. Shabaz of Swaziland is recognized."

"Madame Secretary, how do we know this power outage was not caused by the Texans, and if it was, it would be an act of war that would allow us to respond in kind. We have a major country out of power as well as a rebuff from Texas. If they can rebuff the United Nations, then what power do we have? Speaking for myself and a number of my colleagues, we recommend a retaliatory attack and destroy their oil storage facilities as punishment for their attack on the energy infrastructure of the US."

"Mr. Shabaz, the United States and our people are investigating this outage, and although it is very early in the investigation, the analysis is pointing toward a mishap having to do with the age of the grid. I do, however, agree we must be careful with the appearance of weakness in this situation and need to be strong and forceful in our response. That is why we believe a full blockade on all Texan ports of commerce is the proper step while we assess and help repair the power infrastructure. If we had not had these blackouts, we would have full access to our spy and satellite network as well as more efficient communication to coordinate an attack along their Gulf coast. Much of our military structure and communication is down, so we need to restore those assets before we can be at full capabilities. Does that answer your question, Ambassador Shabaz?"

"Yes, Madame Secretary, I yield my time to Ambassador Herrmoza from Brazil."

Ambassador Herrmoza was a decorated general of Brazil and became the Vice President of Brazil before being appointed to the UN post. "Madame Secretary, there is growing sympathy for the Texan movement in South America. I would just warn you and this chamber of the dangers a long negotiating period could have in our hemisphere. Several of our countries are oil-producing suppliers who have long-term economic relationships with Texas, and they are not firmly on board with this action. Can you guarantee this will be short and decisive action that will not drag on? The public sympathy will not stay on our side for very long."

"Ambassador Herrmoza, and to all the Ambassadors of South America, we have been in communication for a long time with your continent and are very aware of the economic realities of your region. Your people must understand they and their countries have been exploited by the Texan oil industry for decades. When they come into the world community, they will have to share their wealth and make those contracts for your oil more fairly written for your underprivileged countries. Your people must know one of the reasons we are taking this action is for them and their futures. They deserve to share in the wealth of Texas rather than being exploited by them. When Texas does sign this resolution—and, yes, there will be a very short action—we will have the world finally working in unison to solve our shared problems of poverty, starvation, and inequality.

"Yes, Ambassador Wong of China."

"Madame Secretary, we too have been close trading partners with Texas and have built strong alliances, both economically and technologically. We admire much of what they have accomplished, although they are very tough competitors. China agrees with you that we need to make them agree to the resolution and stop the exploitation of small undeveloped countries around the world, and especially in the Asian continent. That said, we also do not want to destroy their ability to provide and produce many of the products they provide efficiently and on time for us and the world. We and many countries rely on their production, as you can see from the blackout. We would prefer this can be negotiated to a satisfactory outcome, but if we do need to use some sort of force, let it be short and swift with as little collateral damage as possible. You need to understand we are walking a dangerous tightrope with the economy of the world. The last thing we need is to fall into another massive depression like 2025."

"Ambassador Wong, you have my word that is exactly what our generals are planning to do. We will only use whatever amount of force is necessary to accomplish the task. We expect this will be a short action, and it will be very surgical, causing as little damage and casualties as necessary. You must also understand if we allow Texas to stare us down, then which country will be next, and who after that until we have no member countries in the United Nations. We need to stand together and make this happen so the Texans will comply quickly rather than trying to wait us out."

Steven Moses looked around the board room, which had a magnificent view of the Texas horizon stretching across the Lone Star landscape for over a hundred miles from the top of Moses Tower. He was never tired of the view. "Ladies and gentlemen, you all know why I called this meeting and the critical nature of it. You have been briefed, and I expect you can tell us what you have found from your departments. As you know, this is a meeting between our Energy, Technology, and Weapons Development groups in hopes of designing a system to protect our energy facilities.

"We need to install more advanced defensive and offensive systems that will protect our facilities from the attacks, which will be coming in the next days and weeks. Ideally, we will be able to protect our refining and shipping ports as well as the production wells off the coast. Those well caps, of course, are mostly below water; and with automatic shutoff valves controlled from here, the damages would be minimal and easily repaired after this is over. We also expect very little attack on our electrical power generation since these will be powering America when we are able to get back on line. So, the main targets will be the oil refining and storage facilities initially. Am I correct, Major General Summers?"

"Yes, that is our assessment. We expect they will attack those oil storage and production facilities first to knock out our primary products and cause the most damage possible to a high-priority target. Our most vulnerable refineries are Offshore Refineries One, Two, and Three. Being built five miles out on twenty-acre platforms makes them inviting targets for their ships and planes. This is a two-edged sword in that it is a small area with a maximum amount of damage per attack, but it is also very defensible in a narrow kill corridor if we can develop and deploy some weapons to defend them.

"The good news is, unless they do something completely out of character militarily, we know exactly where they are coming from, so we can use our target as bait for their weapons. I warn everybody, though, there is an old saying that all of the best-laid plans go out the window after the first shot is fired."

"Thank you, General, and that is sound advice. We are working on those weapons, which is why we invited Bill Branson, our Tech Leader, to tell us what his teams have been working on. Bill."

"Thank you, Steven. Hopefully, we will give the General some mousetraps for his giant piece of cheese. As most of you know, we have been supplying much of the weapons around the world, which were applied to many of the weapons' platforms we produced and other countries have made. Our engineers have been working double shifts since we got the drift of our acquisition by the UN and have made some significant developments with our weapons systems.

"A couple of the defensive upgrades we have developed are advanced digitally protective skins for our fighters and hover jets. Think of them as skins that are computer screens that project the background on that screen. Also, they will deflect any lasers hitting them as well as detection wavelengths. They have multiple advantages since they are a perfect camouflage, blending into whatever background they are against. They simply put the background on the skin and become invisible to the eye as well as to electronic detection.

"We are developing the ability to make a surface digitally protected with a series of lasers to jam any laser weapon on the planet for short periods of time. Our problem is we can only cover limited areas for limited periods of time since this technology uses vast amounts of memory to jam the large numbers of codes that the enemy laser weapons possess. We are trying to miniaturize as much as we can. It will also stealth any guidance systems for conventional bombs with laser targeting. As of now, we have no capability to defend since we haven't deployed any of these weapons yet, and we are completely defenseless to an attack.

"As most of you know, we have retrofitted our F-23s with a ramjet booster to make them a crossover between a jet and a rocket, giving us the fastest aircraft in the world. We are training our pilots and working out the issues with making them maneuverable at these supersonic speeds. We are also working out the details of how our weapons systems work at those speeds. We have made great strides in developing intuitive mind-control targeting, thanks to our gaming industries. We have the best fighter on the planet, without question. It's just that we only have around a hundred of them compared to over twenty thousand UN aircraft. I guess you can say we have them right where we want them."

The room chuckled in appreciation.

Bill Branson continued, "Along those same lines, we have been developing some multi-Mach drones that have been showing great promise. Again, we have not deployed any of these weapon systems or aircraft. We will begin these systems as soon as we finish testing them. Any questions?"

President Stewart spoke first. "I appreciate all you are doing and how hard your men are working, but do we really have time to completely test these weapons since we may be attacked any day now? This rolling blackout will only last a few days, and perhaps a week, and then they will have the ability to attack us."

"I agree, President Stewart," Branson replied. "However, we would be putting people at risk if these are not tested, and we don't have enough man-hours to make things happen any faster. We should have these systems ready to go in two or three weeks and then begin deploying."

Steven rose to speak. "Bill, this is our number one priority. Whatever you must do and whatever it costs, these weapons need to be deployed. I want them completed and deployed in three weeks from today, even if you must use every person at Texas Technologies to get that done. Can we count on you?"

"Yes, sir, I have no idea how, but we will get it done."

June's earpiece rang, and the midair halo display said it was unknown, which meant she knew who it was. "Hello?"

"Professor Darling, Ranger here. I have something you need to know. We made a raid on a prison camp during the electrical blackout, and we found something absolutely unfathomable. There was a camp up in the Adirondacks set up to hold political prisoners, which we raided to help some of our prisoners escape and were expecting to release around twenty thousand or more to help us with our battles in New York. When we broke in, we found a death camp."

"What do you mean by 'a death camp'?"

"Just what you think. It was designed to kill political prisoners. We found less than a thousand people still there and found they were killing over five thousand per month and that there are camps like this scattered around the country. I have a file we made with video and interviews we need you to share with your people and the rest of the world. I am sending that to you when I hang up and hope you pass it to your news distributors to let the world know."

"Ranger, are you telling me there are concentration camps like in Nazi Germany and Mao's China killing people simply because they are politically disagreeing with the government? Are you sure these weren't actually criminals who were guilty of capital crimes, or that the political prisoners were not being transferred somewhere else?"

"No, we found people in the infirmary with IVs of cyanide in their arms who were dead and rows of corpses being prepared for cremation. It was a death factory, and we have the video and interviews to prove it. We… what the—" Just then, the connection went dead.

"Hello! Ranger? Hello!" June frantically tried to reconnect, but the connection could not find the source.

She tried all of her redials and reconnects and searches for a connection—and nothing—causing her to fear the worst. All she could do was wait and hope that his download was sent and could reach her memory base. Were they really killing their enemies in New York? Can that be true? And if it is true, she needed proof to let the rest of the world know. She would wait through the night, but if there were no files in the morning, she knew she would have to go find Ranger. She had a sense he was in real danger, and nobody knew it but her, so she had to help.

The next morning, she checked her memory banks at home and the office, and there was nothing with no messages on her phone, which meant he was either captured or deep underground. Either way, she knew she had to find those files to confirm what Ranger had told her. She rode the shuttle down to the Moses Tower and met Steven for an early breakfast.

He lit up when he saw her, giving her a kiss and a hug as he offered her to sit with him in the executive cafeteria. She ordered an Alaskan crab omelet with a cup of tea while she looked out over the horizon, staring far beyond it.

Steven noticed her distance and quiet mood. "What is it, June? Is something wrong? You seem to be worried about something. Second thoughts about getting married?"

She laughed and shook her head as a tear rolled down her cheek. "I think they have captured Ranger. If they have, it's his death sentence!"

She explained the phone call and everything he had told her about the concentration camps. She told how she waited and worked all night to get his connection back to get the files and find out if he was safe. Steven was in shock as he listened.

"Steven, I have to go to New York and find him and bring him and his files back to get this story out. I contacted the girl who escorted us out of the subways, and she said they are looking for him, too, and have some tips where he might be. I must do this to get the truth out. With this upcoming war, there is no way we can allow this story to be buried. The world needs to know what they are doing and who is doing it."

"Then I'm going with you. I'm not taking a chance of losing you again up there. The last time you went on your own was too close, and I don't know what I would do to lose someone else I love. Besides, we are a team, and I can fly you to places you can't go without me."

"You can't go! They know who you are, and they would be watching your every move, and you have too much to do here. I can go as a journalist who is covering this story and will have a certain amount of anonymity. You would draw attention to me, and that is the last thing Ranger needs right now. There are still domestic flights to New York, and even though they may watch me, I will not be that valuable a target as a professor and a member of the press. And yes, I know, I will be careful. But this story is too big and can destroy their entire smokescreen as a guardian of the oppressed. I have to go and find Ranger and those videos."

"Look, June, everything you say is true, but I need to come with you. I will go as an official ambassador to continue some last-minute negotiations with the UN. This will keep the focus on me and can allow you to be in the meetings as an official reporter, and we can look for Ranger together. Besides, you are recording this for history, and whether we like it or not, I am a big part of this story. I am not going to let you go there again without any help or protection. If there is still a chance to stop this war, we need to take it. If there are death camps being run by their government, it needs to be exposed so the world will know about their existence." He was used to the times when his fame was a hindrance, and this was one of them, except this time, he could be a diversion. She could be found by Ranger's group, and she was the only one they trusted, so she was the only one who could possibly pull this off.

He looked over at her. "We can only go for a week. If we can't find him or the camp in that amount of time, then you're not going to be able to, and things will be getting too dangerous as the war will be imminent. I hate going there in the first place, but we must do this, and they won't be suspecting us, although they will be trying to follow us. I'll use the stealth upgraded Stallion and keep them off our tracks. I had it retrofitted with some upgrades that will be extremely helpful in this situation."

June relented. "I love you for helping, and I really don't know why you put up with me. We need to do this, and bringing anyone else will only endanger them, and we won't be able to get around as easily. I will be there as a reporter who is just trying to get the story at the UN and not draw too much suspicion while you're negotiating. They will be suspicious of us as Texans, but I don't want to be looking like we are there for something else. I know this is dangerous, but we don't have any choice if these camps are real. Why *do* you put up with me? It must be love."

"Must be," as they both laughed.

Captain Thomas was getting the feel of his new jet and was now able to target, maneuver, and fire while entering and leaving ramjet speed. He had learned to bank and change directions faster than any of the other pilots in the training group. It was as if he had always flown this jet and was becoming a part of it as his senses began to adapt to the speed and technology of the fighter. The new advanced lasers were far more powerful than anything he had ever seen and had kill power out to fifty miles. This should give him an advantage of nearly twenty miles over anything the UN had in their arsenal and, with the advanced targeting electronics, will be far more advanced than anything they will be seeing. In today's battles, there is a saying, "Microseconds make the difference between flying, spying, and dying."

They practiced their mock dogfights over the Gulf, knowing in a few days they would be in real air battles protecting Texas and these oil facilities, which they all knew would be the primary targets. They practiced their attacks from over a hundred thousand feet to make full use of their ramjet boosters. This was a riskier attack mode since pulling out going over four thousand miles per hour was difficult, but from a strategic standpoint, with their stealth technology, they would be appearing from space and should be looking at a shooting gallery. The plane shook and groaned every time it bottomed the trough from the heavy G-forces, but the more times he practiced, the better he got until the plane literally floated through the bottom. This may be how they could overcome the huge advantage the United Nations Air Force had in numbers of aircraft.

He saw the attackers on his down screen attacking out of the south. He nosed down, hitting the afterburners shooting past Mach 4. He was slammed back in his seat as the 3D screen filled his windshield while he squeezed the targeting computer as he looked at the various targets. The visual targeting tagged all the aircraft as they lit one after another with hit and kill lights, making their way across the horizon just as he pulled back, feeling those heavy Gs forcing him deep into his seat as the ramjet fired, turning his aircraft into a blur across the Gulf, climbing back to subspace just as the booster cut out well out of the fray. He felt himself going back to conventional as he banked back off the Jamaican beaches, then coasted back to Bush Air Force Base north of Houston.

After he landed, he was called into Commander Jackson's office for his debriefing. As he walked in, he noticed another half dozen generals, who all turned as he entered the room. He knew he was either in big trouble or had done something good to have all those full birds in one place.

"Captain Thomas, enter. I hope you know everyone here, but let's just say we are all very impressed with your flying ability and how you have quickly adapted to our ramjet booster technology. For most of our pilots, it is a bit overwhelming to fly at those speeds with as much information and targeting coming at you, but you seem to thrive on it. What's your secret?"

"I'm not sure, Commander. I think I just have flying in my blood and want to do my part to help Texas. It just seems, Sir, that when I hit those burners and ramjet, suddenly, not only does the plane begin accelerating, but so does my body and mind. It is as if I become a part of their speed and the entire world slows down to normal even though I know we are rocketing through the Machs. It is then when everything becomes clear, and the targets look like they are all moving in slow motion compared to my speed, and they become sitting ducks on a pond.

"Sir, I'm not trying to be cocky. But when I'm up there, it's not like I'm flying at all, but every single muscle and nerve is a part of the control panel, and taking the plane places it never has gone. I have complete confidence in her, and I know it is the best fighter ever developed. I also know these jets are all that is standing between winning and losing this war and our freedom. These few planes may be the only thing standing between thousands or even millions of Texans living or dying. It may be like Winston Churchill said in his wartime speech during the Battle of Britain, 'Never was so much owed by so many to so few,' and I am one of the few. Does that answer your question, sir?"

"Yes, it does, Captain Thomas, and we have been going over your results along with the other pilots who are also impressed with your abilities, some who have been flying for years as fighter pilots. But you have exceeded all their results. We have decided to promote you to Wing Commander so you can begin sharing your skills with the other pilots. Frankly, Captain, you are the best pilot we have seen go through here and are the best pilot we have on the ramjet F-23. So, Captain Thomas, come here and let me pin on your Squadron Commander wings. Along with this comes your Texas citizenship. Congratulations, Texas Air Force Wing Commander Thomas."

Terry Thomas was stunned. Not only was he promoted to being the squad leader, but he now had his dream come true of being a Texas citizen in only two years. He was gob-smacked as he looked up at Commander Davidson saluting him, and he quickly snapped a salute back and shook all their hands. He knew now was not the time to tear up, although he had never been so moved in his life. He walked out of the room, thinking he was already flying higher and faster than any jet he flew. He thought to himself as he walked across the tarmac, *"Captain Terry Thomas, Texan."* His eyes began to well up as he thought how proud his parents would be. That would all have to wait as he headed for postflight drills and breaking down the latest video.

Steven stepped into the Stallion and checked over all the gauges while June looked across the river. He lifted off from La Guardia, heading toward the United Nations Compound. A few minutes later, he and June sat in Secretary-General Polentas' waiting room looking out over the East River, wondering if Ranger was dead or alive. She had to keep that out of her mind as she was about to have the interview of a lifetime between her and the most powerful woman in the world and the man holding the fate of nations in his hands. Does she know about the concentration camps, or is someone on a mission of their own? She wondered if she could get a clue during this interview. The secretary motioned to her and Steve. "Madame Secretary-General will see you now."

Steven's hair on his neck stood on end as his senses moved to a heightened state. He was fully aware that the President of the United States had died in this office under very suspicious circumstances, so he had to be always aware of his and June's safety. He entered the office, and no matter what you thought of the United Nations or New York City, the view of Manhattan from these heights was inspiring. You couldn't see as far as you could from the Moses Tower, but you could see skyscrapers and cityscapes spread across the horizon and stretching out to the Atlantic Ocean.

He looked at the diminutive UN Secretary-General Salinas Margarita Polentas standing and coming around her desk to shake his hand. He noticed standing next to her was Ambassador General Herrmoza of Brazil, who also shook hands and greeted them through cold, squinted eyes—eyes you knew you could never turn your back on.

"Hello, Madame Secretary and Ambassador Herrmoza, you know Professor Darling, who is a journalism professor for the University of Texas and documenting all of our negotiations for historical record, if you don't mind. We wish we were meeting on more friendly terms and are hoping we can ease some of the tension we are all feeling right now."

"We share your hopes, Mr. Moses," she replied. "Things seem to have spun out of control, and we are hoping that in our meetings, cooler heads can prevail, and we can come to an amiable agreement. What exactly brings you here, Mr. Moses?"

"Well, Madame Secretary, the President of Texas has sent me, and we are hoping we can find a way to avert a military solution and be able to maintain our sovereignty which we have worked so hard for generations to acquire."

"What do you propose, Mr. Moses? You have already turned down our final offer for peace and will not join the United Nations as a fully partnered nation, so there doesn't really seem to be another solution unless you have something we have not yet discussed. Do you have something new?"

"Well, yes, Madame Secretary, we are proposing something that we believe can be beneficial to both parties and allow us to begin to work with the UN. What we want to offer is, we will pay half of the United Nations dues you are asking and would renegotiate that in twelve to twenty-four months so we can begin to adapt to some of your regulations and procedures, which would be mutually negotiated. We also believe you can save much of your expenses if you would suspend your regulations and regulators from having to physically come to Texas and maintain our practices. We will send you audited results from our companies on an hourly basis to verify our compliance with our pollution standards.

"As you know, we fall well below the World Pollution Commission mandates for our own emission controls, and there is really no need for you to send all those people to monitor something that is already being taken care of. We have all our industry emission monitoring on the Internet for anyone to look up day or night in real-time. We would also expect to pay our full expenses for the UN protection of the trade routes we use for international commerce. We are hoping these compromises would be satisfactory to avert any military actions which may be considered by this body."

"Mr. Moses, you cannot be serious. Why would we ever agree to not only Texas not becoming a *full* member, but you would most likely *never* become one? This proposal is not acceptable, and if this is all you have, then you are wasting your and my time. Certainly, you did not come all the way from Texas to offer this, did you?"

"Please, Secretary Polentas, of course, we didn't fly up here to waste your time. Just tell me what we can do as an equitable compromise to make this agreement work. You must understand our countrymen are very proud people that value their freedom and liberty. What is it we can offer to potentially give both of us what we want?"

"Well, Mr. Moses, pride is the type of thing that can start wars. Time for compromise is over. The minimum we will accept from you is the complete acceptance as a full member of the United Nations. We have already discussed this in the past, and you should understand this completely. Unless you accept our resolution, we will be putting a full sea and air blockade on your country in one week. I will be announcing this in the morning. Now do you have a more appealing offer?"

"Not currently, Madame Secretary. Let me talk to President Stewart and see what else I can offer you in the morning. Before you make this announcement, I would like one more opportunity to discuss another proposal with you. Can we meet first thing in the morning?"

"Unless you are willing to agree to our resolution, I see no point in carrying these discussions any further."

"With all due respect, Madame Secretary Polentas, we are potentially talking about starting a world war. Surely you would want to exhaust all opportunities to avoid that. I guarantee you, Texas does not want to go to war if we can avoid it. You and I know we have limited resources to fight such a war and do not want to face the possibility of having our fellow Texans killed. We see this resolution as a complete surrender of our sovereignty to the UN and a giving up of our country's independence. This is not acceptable for Texas. You don't seem to understand, we have been proud, hardworking people for over two hundred years, and after we won our secession from the United States, a long-held dream had come true. We were once again a fully sovereign republic.

"We then worked hard to pay off our debt, and through resource development and free-market capitalism, we were able to not only survive but flourish. This has led to the highest standard of living in the world as well as the lowest poverty and best education of any country, anywhere. We have used competition to expand our lead in all areas. You want us and are forcing us through military force to give up our freedom and turn it over to the United Nations. Well, we Texans are not going to give up our freedom willingly and would like to be able to negotiate an arrangement that will allow us to keep what we have built as a country and pay you a reduced tax for reduced monitoring and UN services. Surely you can understand our side of the issue and will give us an opportunity to offer another proposal before you declare an act of war such as a blockade."

"Mr. Moses, we are not the freedom-stealing monsters you portray us. We are simply trying to help as many of the poor and hungry around the world as possible by leveling the playing field. Many of those countries do not have access to the resources and facilities a wealthy country like Texas has. We are simply trying to give more help for the poorer countries and trying to make things fairer and more equal for everyone."

"What would be fair and equitable is to let the free market determine who succeeds and who fails," Steven replied. "That is what is truly fair. You would have, within a generation, a worldwide economic recovery that would truly begin to eliminate hunger and poverty. If you would give us an opportunity, we could teach these countries how to make that happen and begin to see real progress in all those poverty-plagued areas that have been hurting around the world. It isn't their resources or will to work or unfair advantage; it is repressive governments that take the resources and waste them for their own enrichment through political corruption."

Polentas came back, "Not every person or country had a father who passes oil wells and refineries down to their children like you have, Mr. Moses. You may believe the capitalist system is fair when it is anything but fair. Those who have, get rich or stay rich, while those who do not, don't."

Steven was obviously getting angry as he raised his voice, "As you know, Madame Secretary, I made my success from developing a way to extract oil from dry wells, which not only helped me but helped people all around the world with lower oil and energy prices. My invention not only made thousands of people wealthy beyond their dreams but alleviated the pain of the poor around the world to have affordable energy helping them to avoid more pain and suffering. This argument doesn't really accomplish much, and I would ask you to indulge me tomorrow to see if we can make some progress before you begin to use military force."

"Very well. We will meet tomorrow morning at 9:00 a.m. to see if we can avoid an armed confrontation. Ambassador Herrmoza, can you escort them to the hoverport?"

Ambassador Herrmoza escorted them to their hover jet and returned to Secretary Polentas' office. He saw the look of anger in her eyes.

"They are gone. What do you think about tomorrow morning? Are you going to hold off on your announcement for the blockade?"

"No, I doubt he is going to offer anything of value. He's simply trying to stall and has something else up his sleeve. He is a danger to us. He won't negotiate or budge off his position. He is more troublesome than President Chambers and needs to have an accident, just like the President."

168

"I understand, Madame Secretary, that would truly be a shame. New York City is a dangerous place."

THE STORM HITS

Steven and June were walking around the inside of the pockmarked warehouse where he rescued her from the attack. They could see bloodstains on the outside, and it was obvious there was a fierce battle rather than the usual gang fights you would expect in the surrounding neighborhoods. The area had become bleaker than it was when they saw it the first time since the union gangs were completely in control of the city. There were now numerous bodies hanging from lampposts on every corner, giving the city the putrid stench of rotting flesh.

June looked over at Steven. "She said she would meet me here. I hope nothing happened to her?"

"I don't know, but let's see if we can find any clues of who these people were and how the women were able to get down into the subways. That may lead us somewhere. You said they took you through a passageway to get you to the alcove where I found you. Do you remember where that was?"

"We all went to the back of the building over here behind some storage bins. It seemed like they were well hidden, but the worshipers knew exactly where they were and where they went. They were back here in this corner behind these barrels." June searched in the back of the warehouse in a cluttered area that likely wasn't straightened up since the attack, and everything was turned upside down. She found a small door hidden behind some large refrigerator-sized boxes and clutter.

"Steven, come here and help me lift some of this stuff. I think this is where they took me out."

"Here, let me move some of that stuff, and we can get down to that doorway. It looks like the handle is either broken or not working on purpose. Is there anything that we can use to force this door open? Hold on a second; I think I have seen one of these latches before on a rig in Mexico; let me try this. It seems to be jammed."

The handle suddenly began to turn counterclockwise by itself, and the doorway slowly began to open. Blonde-haired women peered around the corner and asked, "June, is that you?" "Yes, are you Susan?" She nodded.

"Steven, this is Susan Bennett, and she is the one who helped us out of the warehouse and through the tunnels to the rescue area you found me."

Susan motioned, "Follow me, and I will take you to the safe house where we have the files and some help. It isn't far."

They bent down as they entered the small entryway, which was about waist high. Steven was glad he brought his flashlight and shined it down into the tunnel. He reached back for June's hand as he crouched in the dark and moved forward, following Susan, who had her own headlamp. They were inching down a pathway inside a false wall, coming down to the end of the warehouse and a dead end.

She then led them down into a stairwell. At the bottom of the stairs was a hatch on the brick floor which appeared to be locked and crossed with a white cast iron handle that was partially exposed.

Steven turned the handle and pulled it up, exposing another set of stairs heading into the darkness. They quickly walked down the steps that led to the New York sewer system. The sewage smell and humidity hit their nostrils like a day-old skunk kill on a hot Texas highway. When they reached the bottom of the stairs, the tunnels went four separate directions with worn trails in the raised brick shoulders.

"Follow me and stay close behind; this is very treacherous walking," she said, pointing to a darkened tunnel heading east toward the river.

They walked cautiously along the brick walkways near walls while the water and sewage flowed inches from their feet, heading toward the treatment facilities. The smell and darkness were like an invisible umbrella engulfing them in an eerie cloud. The flashlight barely lit up twenty feet, but it was just pure smelly darkness after that. You could almost see the smell rising off the acrid water. As they rounded a corner, they could hear some men off in the distance echoing through the tunnels. They couldn't tell which tunnel it was coming from, but it sounded like a large group of men.

Susan and Steven turned off their lights and moved quietly toward the voices. June held on to the back of Steven's shirt, trying not to breathe as she tried to feel the bricks along the wall and under her feet while not making noise or falling into the water flowing beside them. There was no way to tell if they were friends or foes, but there was only one way to find out. They moved closer and closer, trying to make out what they were saying. As they inched nearer, the words became clear.

"The boss said we need to clean up these neighborhoods before they can declare martial law. There's no way we can continue to fight the resistance while we're trying to maintain order in the city. If we could finally get the Christians under control, we'd finally have New York working properly. We have them pushed out of Brooklyn, but they're still well established in Queens. At least we got that pesky Ranger. We won't be having any trouble from him again." They all laughed and nodded at that comment.

June and Steven looked at each other. He whispered, "Maybe they'll give us a clue of where he is or if he's still alive? Let's move a bit closer."

As they peered around the corner, they could make out a large group of men lit in the dingy, dark tunnel that widened out and was lit by some work lights for the subway. Some were smoking, and others had their union jackets and hats on with a large Italian man who was obviously the leader doing most of the talking.

"We've been given some special orders to rid them of some other pests. As you know, that oil baron puke from Texas has been a thorn in our side, and we need to take him to the same place upstate; we took the Ranger to put on ice. Jeff, I want you and your boys to make this guy disappear just like you did our other problem. The bounty on him is double what you received for the Texas Ranger."

Jeff whistled and said, "Tell your friends we appreciate their generosity, and soon they'll be sharing the same cell."

"Tommy, you keep rounding up the Christians. They've been hitting our supplies hard, and you need to stop them. Like we always say, the only good Christian is a hanging cross, and we need more hanging crosses!" That brought another round of laughter and clinking of beers.

Susan, Steven, and June began backing away from the group. June was shaking from head to toe but needed to get out of there before they were seen. As they were backing up, two rats came scurrying out of a hole and startled them, causing June to make a muffled scream.

The group stopped talking and looked their way. "Who was that?" Tommy yelled.

They started running back up the tunnel, and the group of men started after them. Steven was pulling on June's hand, trying to keep her running in the right direction while his light barely made out the small ledge they were running on. Just as they were rounding the last corner to reach the stairs back up to the warehouse, someone came flying out of the darkness and caught Steven square in the ribs, driving him into the water. More men came in behind and held him underwater, trying to drown him. June and Susan began screaming as they let him up and began punching him in the face and stomach until he slumped back into the water.

The men began walking their captives back to the meeting. As they came into the light, the leader had a look of surprise and said, "Well, well, look what we got here. We didn't even have to go find him—he came right to us like a mouse to cheese in a trap. Jeff, you and your boys just got yourselves another big bonus. This is the richest man in the world, Mr. Steven Moses. All the money in the world ain't going to help you now, Mr. Big Oil Money!"

Jeff walked up and gave Steven a look of disgust and punched him in the stomach once more, bending him over as he tried to catch his breath through blood-covered lips. He grabbed Steven by the head, holding it while he kneed him in the face sending him sprawling on the ground while his nose and mouth exploded with blood. "You rich guys ain't so tough when your bodyguards aren't around, are you?"

Stazi Ramone barked, "Stop that, we have to have the goods in decent shape if we want to get our reward. If anybody else touches them, you're answering to me! So, clean him up and make sure he doesn't have any weapons. Let's take him over to the boss at the UN. They will have a nice surprise for him. Make sure you have him and the girl secure while you clean them up. Hold this other one here and try her, then hang her for trying to help these spies. We don't want anybody to notice when we take these two upstairs. So, Jeff, you going to take your wife on a cruise with all this reward money?"

They dragged him between two men, with June following in the grasp of another through the tunnels until they reached a subway station and walked him up the stairs. When they made it up to the street, they had a man on each side and two in front and back; but they didn't want to look like they were kidnapping him, so they held him loosely while June was being escorted behind them. They just looked like a couple of homeless people covered in filth.

Steven could see the van they were heading for with the Dockworkers' emblem on it. He slowly slid his hand on top of his belt buckle and pushed the button on his hidden remote hover key. This activated the emergency GPS retriever on the Black Stallion, making it take off and come flying over the top of the building directly to the right of them and barreling across the street straight for them in silent mode.

Steven saw it coming directly at them as he slowly lowered himself into a crouch like he was beginning to pass out while it bowled over the two lead bodyguards. He threw his shoulder into the one on his right and punched Jeff on his left with a shot he hadn't thrown since his days at the Wildcatter Brew and Pub, dropping him like the last cowboy he caught insulting Sandy when they were dating. He dropped him like a sack of potatoes, opening a lane of escape.

This shocked the group for a moment. He grabbed June and threw her into the Black Stallion with himself right behind and hit the throttle as the doors closed shut. Within twenty seconds, they were out of sight and flying over the Atlantic, leaving his captors in the jet wash. Stazi's men picked themselves up and asked each other what had just happened while they tried to wake their boss from his knockout punch.

Steven looked over at June, catching his breath, and declared, "How do you like our date in New York City so far? We better not go back to our hotel since they'll be waiting for us. We'll find a place out of the city where we should be safe."

"What about Susan?"

"There's nothing we can do. We have no idea where they've taken her and can only pray she gets away."

June looked out over the ocean at the melting darkness. There was a silent, calming beauty to the boats bouncing toward their home ports while their lights flickered in the dusk. She could see most of the seaboard from their height, stretching from the boardwalk of Atlantic City all the way up to Providence.

Even though she knew she was now a hunted person, she felt comfort knowing she was with Steven, who she saw in another light after their escape. He wasn't the calm and reserved business negotiator she had come to know, but he had a rugged side that was protective and manly. The first escape was not a fluke; this is who he is. She leaned over and laid her head on his shoulder and let the warmth of the night drift; her eyelids closed as her dreams spread peacefully just behind their covers.

Captain Thomas and his wingman, Firefly, were flying reconnaissance over the Gulf. He was monitoring the military ships moving into the Texas shipping lanes. He had been watching thirty-four combat ships fanning out across the Gulf. He was taking computer readings on their size, speed, and weapons. Most were cruiser class from all nations around the world, although the largest group were US ships, which included a carrier group with some of their latest aircraft. He had no idea if the jamming and stealth technology of his F-23 would be able to counter their detection, although he had a hunch he would be finding out soon.

He continued with his mission of getting computer signatures of the Carrier UNN Kofi Annan, making sure he stayed out of its fifty-mile shoot-down zone. His stealth-tronics said the carrier's counter laser was attempting a contact, although they were not able to get a lock on him. He knew their techs were going crazy. They could tell someone was sweeping their ship from somewhere and were doing everything they could to trace it back to the source. Just then, his alarms went off, and maximum stealth systems switched on as his warning showed aircraft closing on him from his nine o'clock. His radio broke silence with Firefly screaming, "Let's get out of here, Rattler! They found us so let's hit the deck and get back home."

"Roger that!" He pushed full throttle, kicking in the afterburners, hitting the deck below the sensors, and banked back north toward home, knowing this would give the carrier a brief signature, but he was found anyway from aircraft. The bogeys followed him, sweeping him the entire ten minutes while he was able to sweep their system, both knowing if this was a shooting match, one or both would be spinning into the Gulf. This should be some great signature data for his boys back in the Spook's Cave, even if he was a bit peeved, they were found. He knew there had to be a hole in the laser masking if they were able to spot him before he could spot them, which better be corrected. The good news is he didn't let them find out about his ramjet, which he knew he would reveal to them at the proper time. The only thing he was focused on now was skimming the waves and getting back to Bush Field safely without revealing his entire stealth system.

Steven and June found the little bed and breakfast called the White Pine Inn in the Adirondacks that he mentioned earlier. They checked on the net, and the inn guaranteed no Internet or phone services. He thought they would have the best chance of not being recognized there and not reported. It was a cute little log lodge design with four bedrooms overlooking a small pond. It had individual cabins scattered across the grounds. He rented two cabins on the lake near the lodge since they didn't seem to have many renters. Although he never slept, he stayed up and used the Black Stallion GPS satellite service to identify three locations south of Syracuse that were potential prisons that could be holding Ranger. June, on the other hand, looked absolutely stunning to him as she walked into the lodge. She obviously had a good night's sleep. She gave Steven a cheery good morning and a peck on his cheek.

"Good morning, hero! How did you sleep? I slept like a princess up in this crystal mountain air."

"Good morning, sweetheart. Hero? I don't know about that, but thanks anyway. I couldn't sleep, so I stayed up and did some satellite searching and found a few locations, which may be one of the prisons Ranger told you about."

"I thought we came here because you can't get any service up here?"

"Anytime I am within five hundred yards of the Black Stallion, I have communication anywhere in the world. So, I used my time last night to look at these sites. I gave a call back to Texas to tell them what was happening and got some updates for my software. We can fly over the top of the potential spots this morning, get some close-up video, and see what we can find. After all, we're not going to be having breakfast at the UN this morning, so we may as well use our time wisely. Now, what are you hungry for?

Stazi Ramone was not thrilled about the meeting with the Ambassador and looked around the opulent office nervously. He was not looking forward to explaining how his men let the most wanted man in the world slip through their fingers. Shelton didn't look much better as they sat in the Secretary General's waiting room.

"The Secretary-General will see you now, gentlemen. Follow me." The secretary led them back to the impressive office overlooking the East River. The room was filled with a dozen men and Ambassador Hermosa, Secretary-General Polentas, as well as a number of assorted Ambassadors and military officers.

Ambassador Herrmoza addressed them, "Gentlemen, you have put us in a very difficult position since you now have exposed our connection with your unions to Mr. Moses. We were expecting to have one of two things happening this morning. Either he was going to be caught and simply disappear, or he would be here this morning to negotiate the treaty and avoid the sea blockade of Texas. Now we have neither option available, and he has vanished. We haven't picked up any detection of his hover jet. How did you idiots manage to let him escape?"

Stazi Ramone responded. "We thought we had him and were taking him to the van to bring him here, but he had some sort of autopilot attack software on his hover jet that knocked down a couple of our men. In the confusion, he was able to get in and escape. I have never seen an aircraft knock somebody off their feet and then set itself to make an escape. Who would have thought that could happen? We were caught completely off guard."

Secretary-General Polentas walked from around her desk and shrieked, "Who would have thought of that? You are bringing in the richest man in the world, and you are not expecting the unexpected? You men have no idea how difficult a position you have put me in. This has forced my hand, which means we are going to have to begin to enforce the blockade today. Major General Mohamed Almach, can your technicians find a single hover jet here in New York City—that is, if he is even in the area now?"

The Major General stood up. "Madame Secretary, we had been tracking it from the time it arrived in La Guardia to the UN yesterday and out to Brooklyn. However, when it made the maneuver during their escape, it engaged some sort of stealth with a laser-detection scrambling technology we had never seen. When we hit it with our lasers and radar, it shows over fifty aircraft in locations spread over a hundred miles and traveling in a hundred different directions. The targets moved around our screens randomly and would simply drop off until they all disappeared. We had no idea which one was him. So, he could be anywhere from Boston to Philadelphia from what we're tracking. Our teams were using everything we had to find it—from satellites to lasers—and we simply could not find it.

Captain Thomas was flying at ninety thousand feet with two squadrons of ten fighters working as two wings spread over fifty miles. He could see the contrails of the commercial aircraft below him as well as the wakes of the numerous ships moving in every direction. At this height, you could still make out the tiny triangles of the ships spread across the Gulf. He could see on his heads-up laser that some of those small triangles were the two carrier groups working the Gulf practicing war games preparing for the upcoming war.

He looked over at his two squadron captains and spoke into his mask, "Okay, Firefly and Sagebrush, let's take a run at those two flattops on our screens—but make sure not to be too threatening. Follow me, boys, and try to stay in a tight formation."

Steven and June were searching the forests of northern New York and soon discovered searching for a settlement or prison in the mountains was like trying to find a flea on a black dog. They flew over the first two suspected locations on the computer. The first was shuttered tight and turned out to be an abandoned work camp. The second was a closed-down hardwood mill. They flew across the hills, looking at the thousands of lakes and forested areas, getting readings of small groups of people but nothing sizable. With one small hover jet, it was a monumental task knowing he would have to be on top of the prison to find it, and he had one potential site left. They looked across the mountains, wondering if people out there knew what was going on in the city, or were they completely tuned out from the world?

Just then, the heat sensors flashed, revealing a large population under them even though there was nothing on the maps or satellite imagery. June and Steve looked at each other in surprise, and she asked, "What do you think that is? It isn't a town or a city. Can we go down and take a closer look? Maybe it's the prison."

He nodded and circled back over the area to get a closer look. He turned the Stallion to silent mode and put the stealth on maximum deflection, then hovered close to treetop level to see what they could find. From a satellite, there would be no detection of the Black Stallion as the upper skin was a computer screen that would show a video of the ground and trees beneath and the sky when looking from below the hover.

It didn't appear to be a prison, although there were lots of tents and temporary structures, so it could be a work camp of some sort. He used the high-zoom cameras to see what he could make out, but there didn't seem to be any real structures or modern technology you would expect from a work camp or prison.

The sensors indicated there appeared to be over two thousand people living in these temporary units. They came around to the south and rose from behind the largest hill to get a better look at the main building where the people seemed to be congregated and aimed their camera on the largest building in the center of the clearing. As the camera focused on it, they looked at each other, puzzled by what they saw. It was a large log structure that appeared to be over a hundred feet long and eighty feet wide. The roof was covered with Mylar, making it invisible to overhead cameras and satellites. Gunshots sounded behind them, and bullets began zipping past them, with a couple bouncing off the Kevlar skin, telling him he had been detected and determined a threat.

"Let's hope they don't have anything with some punch," Steven exclaimed.

He quickly dropped down in an evasive maneuver, building speed from his jets to slingshot the Stallion up and out of the fire zone. They quickly climbed to fifteen thousand feet out of the range of anything they may have. He replayed the video, and as clear as could be, you could see the cross on the log structure. He looked over at June, who was staring at the video in amazement.

She looked up and said, "There are Christians down there. We haven't seen a cross since we left Texas, so we must go back and find out who they are and if they can help. They may be part of Ranger's church and can help us find him."

"I know, honey, but we have to check out the last location, which is about a half-hour away. We can come back and hopefully not get shot. We'll have a better chance of getting in at dark than now. I think we need to figure out how to get in without becoming a target. That said, I really think we may have found a good lead on where Ranger is. I have it marked, and we'll scout it when we get back."

Secretary-General Polentas entered the Grand Chamber to a standing ovation. The chamber was filled with overflowing with every ambassador attending this historic event. The back wall was filled with cameras as the news feeds from every country were represented. You could see the network anchors up in their boxes, introducing the Secretary-General to their audiences.

She stepped to the podium with the two small microphones extending out toward her mouth. She began her speech. "Ambassadors, delegates, leaders, dignitaries, and we especially reach out to the people of Texas to whom I would like to say; we have arrived at a time the United Nations did not want to reach. We believed we could find an agreement with the Texas President and Senate, but they have rejected our multiple offers, and there is nothing more we can do to bring them to the negotiating table. They have abandoned the Texan people and are pushing us toward military action. We even tried to avoid this action with a last-minute meeting with industrialist Steven Moses yesterday but have not heard from him today even though we had a deadline for this morning. From his absence, we have been forced to move forward with an action we have tried to avoid.

"Starting tonight at midnight, Greenwich Mean Time, we will begin a full naval and air blockade of the Texas sea and airports. We will not be allowing any military and commerce ships or aircraft in or out of Texas in an effort to bring them back to the negotiating table. We will also be closing all rail lines except for humanitarian supplies. We in no way plan on harming the people of Texas from receiving necessary food and water, but we will stop any shipments that contain commercial goods or weapons. All ships attempting to leave or enter Texan ports will allow a full inspection by United Nation's ships, and any resistance will be considered an act of provocation and will be responded to accordingly. Any flights outside the Texas borders will be considered an act of aggression and an international act of war.

"This action has been approved unanimously by the Security Council as well as the full assembly. Hopefully, these actions will have a short duration, and we can move forward with the incorporation of Texas into the world Family of Nations. We welcome any discussions that will lead to the immediate agreement of Texas joining this world community. I know I speak for the entire Union of Nations when I say we hope this action will end quickly and peacefully—my phone will always be open. Thank you very much, and continued peace around the world."

The room was solemn in its silence as the Ambassadors quietly sat in their seats, wondering what the next move would be. The Secretary-General and her entourage filed out in a somber procession as they walked to the Security Council chambers.

Captain Thomas was cruising at fifty thousand feet across the Gulf with his two four-plane squadrons when a voice came over the headset, "All aircraft and shipping in the Gulf of Mexico, now hear this: This is the UNN Carrier Kofi Annan, and we are declaring an international blockade of all shipping and flights, both military and domestic, beginning tonight at twenty-four hundred Greenwich Mean Time. We are ordering all ships and aircraft to return to their ports and bases to avoid any conflict. We are taking this action according to international laws within the United Nations Charter. We recommend any military aircraft leave the area and stay grounded immediately. Thank you for your full cooperation."

Captain Thomas called the airbase for confirmation, although they had been expecting this announcement for weeks. "Hello, headquarters, this is Rattler. Do you copy?"

"Yes, Rattler, we copy."

"Is the announcement of the air and naval blockade legitimate?"

"Yes, it is, and you are ordered to land immediately. We do not want to start an international incident."

"Yes, sir, and we will be heading in as soon as we can get turned around. We are pinched between these two carrier groups and will need to keep a wide berth while we maneuver back to the base without being detected."

"That's an affirmative, Rattler. Make it back to base as soon as you can return safely, and keep your eyes and ears peeled. Make sure to follow all the protocols as you have been trained. We are no longer in peacetime."

"Copy that. Over and out."

Captain Thomas and his squadron continued flying south between the two carrier groups, planning to roll west and come back around along the Panama coast. As they were making their turn, their passive displays lit up, showing they had been detected by the ships and fighters coming from the east and closing.

"Squadrons, climb out of here, and let's get up above them and move away." Just as they began climbing, their alarms went off, indicating lasers were being lit and hitting the sides of their planes but were foiled by their deflection technology.

"Change your deflection frequencies and go to multiplier mode. Hit the ramjets!"

Rattler hit his ramjet booster to gain altitude and get up to Mach 7 as he rolled over and dove through the displayed laser mazes. As he dove, he could tell there was no focus by the navel weaponry as they were shooting randomly. He dove for the carriers and began lighting up fighters as he dove down, knowing he could see them, but they were blind to him. His speed was above anything he had ever attempted as the deck was screaming at him.

The carriers and support ships were firing their lasers as well as Sidewinders and Phalanx guns using shoot-and-hope mode. He looked down through the fountain of lights and fire as he went in for the big prizes. He flew by visual intuition, letting the plane become a part of his mind for his final maneuver, which wanted to pull the plane and him apart.

He was diving at Mach 8 when he began to pull up, releasing his array of lock-and-leave ordinances while the plane structure was vibrating and groaning from the stress of the maneuver. As he skimmed the waves and slingshot his jet back into the clouds, he saw the reflection of the explosions hitting their targets. His squadron came in behind him, finishing the support ships and the few aircraft left in the sky. The air and water were empty of military ships and planes.

As they turned back home, they were able to see the results of their fifteen seconds of aggression. Every ship was sinking, and only perhaps sixty minutes separated these giant ships from their watery grave. He never in his wildest imaginations could believe these planes had the power they had when they passed the speed of the defensive algorithms of these warships. These speeds made missiles obsolete, and lasers had no effect on his deflection skins. The only possible weapon was a bullet that was lucky enough to hit the plane. At those speeds, it would tear it apart. This was avoidable with the flight assist computers.

He called the Texas Coast Guard to send rescue ships. Although he was surprised at the power of his fighters, he was keenly aware of the fact he was now at war with the world, and they would be looking for retribution. He could also see the desperation below him as thousands of men and women were heading to the same watery tomb as their crippled ships.

Steven set his Black Stallion down a quarter mile to the south of the camp, where they saw the people they believed were Christians. He scanned the ground for human activity as the sensors showed them still in the camp and scattered around but nothing in this quadrant, which was hidden by some dense forest. He landed in silent mode, making sure to get in and see exactly what this camp was about. He and June exited the Black Stallion and quietly made their way toward the compound.

When they closed within a dozen yards of the first building, they crouched behind it and looked around at the grounds. It was well lit with scattered overhead lights, and the trails were all marked with solar ground lights. They could see families walking together, and almost everyone was headed for the main building with the bronze cross on top.

He suddenly had an idea, grabbed June's hand, and pulled her around the waist, and began walking toward the building with the rest of the families while looking at the ground. She caught on and simply began some idle chitchat with her hand on his shoulder. They walked together toward the main building, up the stairs, then into the back of the building, and off to a side hallway out of the main traffic while nodding to the people. They found a darkened spare room they could hide without being detected.

June whispered to Steven, "That was a gutsy move, hiding in the middle of a crowd. Now what?"

"We need to find out if this is the Ranger's church or a branch of the church. We should be able to hear everything that's going on in there."

He was right. The music started, and the gathering began singing *Amazing Grace*, followed by several old gospel hymns they both grew up with. After a brief set of announcements, the pastor came to the main stage and gave a powerful message on individual freedom and responsibility given only through Jesus Christ and the Holy Spirit. Finally, he mentioned the Texas Christian Fellowship as he finished his sermon. At that point, Steven grabbed her hand again and said, "This is enough for me these people are our friends; let's go meet them."

"Okay, if you think it's safe?"

She was frightened but had faith God had delivered them to this church. They walked together through the back of the auditorium. It was large with cathedral ceilings and stained-glass windows sparkling from the setting sun while they walked up the aisle. The pastor looked down at them and then recognized Steven. His eyes went wide and bewildered at the same time. He was just under six feet tall with light brown hair and a demeanor that was cheerful yet serious. He tried to say something and could barely get the words out, "Are you Steven Moses, and what are you doing here in our church?"

"Yes, I am, and this is my fiancée, June Darling. We came up here to try to find the Texas Ranger, but we were captured last night by a union gang. We were able to escape and have been searching for the prison where they may be keeping him when we found your compound. We found our way inside, and after we heard how Spirit-filled this church was, we decided to come out and meet you."

"Yes, we are part of the Texas Christ Church of New York, and I am Pastor David. We have been searching for Ranger, too. We believe we've found him in prison about a hundred miles from here on the Canadian border. We hope he's still alive, and we're planning a rescue attempt in two days. We can give you details later, but we would be honored if you had a few words to say."

Steven walked up on stage and looked over the crowd of desperate faces. "Brothers and Sisters in Christ, I have to praise God we found you, and I am honored to be with so many Christians standing up in the face of persecution. How many of you were in the warehouse June was in when you were attacked?"

Several hands went up.

"I want to thank you for protecting her, and we're glad you were able to escape that battle. We are on the brink of war. We heard this morning that the UN was placing a blockade on Texas, and I can guarantee you the Texan people are not going to tolerate this type of outward force. Just like everyone in this church, we are not the type of people who are going to roll over and go along with the shutting down of our livelihoods."

"We came up here to try to accomplish two things. One was to find Ranger since he was supposed to send some files to June when his phone suddenly went dead. We were afraid he was captured and came up here to find out. The second reason was to attempt to work out a negotiation with the UN, which would avoid this war from starting. We met with Secretary-General Polentas yesterday and made no progress. We were supposed to meet with her this morning, but we were captured last night while we were searching for you. We managed to escape while they were taking us to the UN for who knows what and began looking up here for a prison or work camp holding Ranger. Sadly, one of your members, Susan Bennett, was captured with us, and they took her to possibly hang her.

"Folks, we are the very last vestiges of freedom. If we are defeated, then freedom is defeated, and it will be decades, if not centuries, before it returns. You have lived under a totalitarian government for almost a decade now, and if they force Texas under their control, then all hope for liberty is completely lost. This is what we're fighting for here, and when we go back to Texas at the end of the week, it is what we will be working toward there.

"America changed when there were more people who wanted to be ruled than those who wanted to be free men. Once those who wanted to be ruled outnumbered those who wanted individual freedom, the entire country had no choice except to be ruled. As the government got larger and more powerful, it restricted more freedoms to where you are now living under a totalitarian world government.

The Republic of Texas

"The countries like America are no longer sovereign but continue to be subjects to this corrupt world dictatorship. You are no more than slaves to the UN and must submit yourselves to its authority with little or no debate while they make all the decisions and mandate regulations. In the end, there is only one way to begin the first steps of freedom, and that is separation and independence from the UN.

"We are with you, and I am sure I speak for all Texans when I say your courage and strength make us proud to stand with you in this fight for freedom around the world. Let me just say, don't mess with Texas, and God bless America!"

In the back of the church, a group began singing the *Star-Spangled Banner*. The chorus began ringing throughout the building as they sang all four verses, louder and prouder than the previous, bringing goosebumps and tears to the entire room.

As they were beginning to leave, a deacon came to the microphone and excitedly made an announcement. "There has been an attack in the Gulf of Mexico. It just came across the net, and the details are still sketchy, but it appears several United Nations ships, including two aircraft carriers, were sunk by the Texas Air Force. The war has begun!"

Captain Thomas sat in an after-action room filled with generals and colonels, waiting to hear what he and his fellow pilots had to say. The news of this victory spread around the world and certainly through the Texas military moments after the attack was a success. The offensive and defensive systems worked well beyond their wildest expectations. The technological superiority was dramatic, and the brass wanted to find out the details.

Commander Jackson began the questioning, "Captain Thomas, what exactly started the attack?"

"Commander Jackson, it all happened so quickly we did not have any time to think, but looking over the recordings, we have reconstructed the attack. When the blockade was announced, my squadron was running maneuvers identifying aircraft as we were flying between the two carrier groups—the UNN Kofi Annan and the UNN Fidel Castro—so we continued in an attempt to get south to some open water. Captain Jameson on my wing and I were both painted by the Carrier Annan and an unidentified enemy aircraft. We were then hit with some lasers, which is when I ordered the switch over to the multiplier stealth and to counterattack. We had no idea if they were going to knock us out of the air or how well our technology would work. Once we switched over and hit the ramjets, we had around fifteen seconds when everything happened before it was over. Once we gained altitude to escape the bogeys, we simply turned over and attacked at a sixty-five-degree angle and could see with our laser illumination they were not aiming at us but using a random scatter, hoping to detect or hit anything. You could easily make out the path to take, and it was simply a matter of the computers dodging the tracers for the track in, then releasing the lock-and-leave ordinances."

Air Force General Brighton asked, "Captain Thomas, you said you were identified and hit by lasers. We have verified that by the marks on your aircraft as well as the data collection. Have you or your techs found out how they were able to defeat our basic stealth software or diffusers?"

"Yes, General. The techs are telling me from their initial findings the enemy had randomly found a hole in our disrupter software. While we have been upgrading for the possibility of war, there is a lot of basic systems upgrading, which has not been completed, and this software was part of it. Once we clicked over to the newer upgrade, we were able to hide ourselves again, and you could see that they went completely blind as to where we were."

Commander Jackson responded, "Captain Thomas, once again, I have to commend you on your resourcefulness in the counterattack. We have never used the ramjet before. How do you feel it responded?"

"Commander, I know it's early in this war and the use of our ramjet F-23 fighter, but I don't believe there is an aircraft that can stand up to this plane. The proof is on the bottom of the Gulf, and we could have caused more damage if we didn't call the attack off almost immediately after our first run. Between the different stealth and weapons technology plus the speed and agility of this aircraft, we may have air superiority which puts you at a distinct advantage in this war. They now have two real choices, to send untold numbers of aircraft and ships at us or use ballistic missiles. We need to be prepared for both since we are completely outnumbered, and they will eventually destroy enough of our weapons to organize an attack on the country. We need to keep bringing ramjet fighters on line and boost our antimissile capabilities, begging your pardon, sir."

"No, Captain, don't bother. This is an open discussion, and you are making especially important points. We do have to prepare for war and be prepared for any contingency. Our large victory changes the dynamics of this war in both the timing and execution. They and we have just realized how large a technological distance we have between each other."

Secretary-General Polentas met with her military cabinet to receive a briefing of the attack and loss of the aircraft carriers Kofi Annan and Fidel Castro. Her top generals were at the table, including Naval Admiral Romelov of Russia, Air Force General Davis from the United States, and Ambassador Herrmoza.

The Secretary-General brought the committee to order and asked, "How did this happen? We had every ship with the highest technology tracking these planes, and they were able to destroy our entire Atlantic Carrier Fleet?"

Admiral Romelov responded, "This was the largest attack on the UN Navy in the history of our government. The speed and strength of the attack were beyond anything we had seen or heard Texas had in their arsenal. We are trying to recreate the attacks on the recovered data, but it appears they may have found a way to put a ramjet engine on their fighters that gave them the ability to hit those kinds of speeds. There was no way for our defense matrices to adjust to the attack. It was over in less than thirty seconds. The survivors said they identified a hostile jet, locked on it, and delivered direct laser hits. Then it changed its stealth frequency and simply disappeared. They described the stealth as suddenly there were hundreds of targets on their screens going all directions. Then out of nowhere, they were being attacked by invisible aircraft that began hitting their ships with laser-guided smart bombs, which were devastating at the speeds they were traveling. They went to the bottom of the ships where they detonated, vaporizing the bottoms of our hulls."

Air Force General Davis added, "Our technicians have been pouring over the data, and it is disturbing. We, too, had a brief signature on these aircraft when they both accelerated beyond anything we are capable of and simply disappeared off our screens, as has been said, multiplying into hundreds of crafts. Unless we can solve this advantage, we are sending our assets to certain death. You cannot see them visually due to their masking stealth technology; you can't pick them up on laser; and if you do get a hit, they simply change to their multiplying program, and you can't guess where they may be. Other than the fact we have them outnumbered by over a thousand to one, we are at a disadvantage by a large distance. We may have to rely on our cruise missile assets to get through their defenses.

"Their final advantage is their speed. We have the tracking on the ones which attacked us, which showed them reaching Mach 7.5 on their attack runs. We know they have been perfecting their ramjet engines and have incorporated them into their fighter jet arsenal, but our engineers cannot understand how they're doing this. They do not understand how they can carry and deploy weapons at those speeds or how the craft holds together at the bottom of the run. By their calculations, it is physically impossible to do what they did, but they did it. We really don't have a counter to these jets since, at those speeds and stealth, we are attempting to shoot down ghosts. We are working on how to break through their stealth, but it is very advanced."

Ambassador Herrmoza finished up, "Secretary-General, this is a critical time in this action. We're not even a day into it, and we're seeing we have no advantage against these Texans in conventional weapons. We can bring more planes and ships into the area, but they will be at risk of being destroyed, and frankly, we cannot afford to lose any more carriers since the time to construct is more than we have. I would suggest we park our ships out of their range and use our cruise missiles to counterattack their port and airports to ground their military and commerce.

"We should start with the oil production and refining capabilities. We can easily reach them from anywhere in the United States or our missile bases in Cuba, and we can use bomber-deployed cruise missiles. They can launch from a thousand miles out and hit their targets. The Texans may be able to shoot down some, but they will never get all of them, and we can pinpoint target their production assets. We need to make a statement after such a devastating attack."

Secretary-General Polentas inserted, "We need these Texans to pay for what they did. Until we do, the world will be waiting and questioning our authority and strength. We need to develop technology to defeat these fighters so we can knock them out of the sky."

Ambassador Herrmoza concluded, "While we're working on defeating their technology, we can overwhelm them with our sheer numbers. We outnumber their fighters by the thousands, and we can take them down by wearing them down, one by one. If they're using ramjet technology, it will only work for a few minutes at a time and then will fall back to conventional. This is when we attack and take them out one at a time. We'll lose lots of our fighters, but it will be worth it to take out these weapons. If they're flying, they have a distinct military advantage."

Secretary-General Polentas wrapped up. "We also need to send a message immediately that we are serious and will not take these attacks— that we'll look at other options we may bring to bear. I want you men to get together and come up with a comprehensive plan to win this war, and I want that plan in the morning. I want these Texans to pay for this."

THE WIND'S RAGE

Steven and David Goldstein were flying in the Black Stallion over the suspected prison site holding Ranger. He had it in silent mode with the full stealth invisibility, which made it very unlikely they would detect him. Just to be safe, he was hovering over a thousand feet up and was scanning the grounds with the thermal sensors. They noticed the guard towers were only half-filled, and it seemed there were not very many guards or prisoners in the prison compound if it was indeed what they were looking at. If Ranger was taken here, it was unlikely he was down there, which made Steven think the worst possibility. He circled back to where the assault team was preparing to attack just east of the compound. He quickly landed and moved over to where the assault team had gathered.

David jumped up on a raised beam and addressed his men, "We just scouted this facility and have some mapping laid out to help you enter where we have found some weaknesses. These two towers here on the northeast side of the compound are not staffed, and you should be able to gain entrance through this fence. We have trained you on how to get through this fence, and once in, you need to go straight for the prison barracks on the south edge and the two next to it, which is where we detected people who we expect are the prisoners. We need to be ready for anything since these guards are war-ready and will be shooting to kill. I will be flying with Steven, and we will give you real-time information of what is going on in the towers on two-way and what the guards are doing on the ground. Let's say a prayer—and start the attack on our signal."

Steven and David climbed into the hover and took off again over the prison. He lowered it down next to the guard towers silently and brought the Stallion within five feet of the east tower, where two guards were looking out over the darkness with a complete lack of interest. The early morning had them off their peak performance even if they could see them. Steven set the hover laser on stun and fired at both guards simultaneously, knocking them both to the floor.

David called to the assault team, "Begin the attack. It's all clear on the east tower. The entire east wall is unguarded, and we will give support suppression fire for your assault."

The men cut through the wire fence using metal cutting lasers, making holes big enough for two or three to go through at the same time. This set off the security alarms, but the towers were now empty as all the guards were either stunned or dead. The ones coming out of the main control center were being cut down by both the Stallion and the first wave of attackers coming through the wire laying down suppression fire. The battle on the grounds only lasted a few minutes before it went inside the complex for a short time, where the leaders called out the "all clear."

Steven turned off the stealth deception software as he landed and headed inside to help find Ranger.

General Davis was addressing Secretary-General Polentas on the conclusions they had come to after working all night on the solutions. "Madame Secretary, we have some difficult decisions to make as we have some complicated issues with the attack by the Texas Air Force. They have some very advanced technology, and as we detailed with you yesterday, much of it is more advanced than our weapons. Our biggest concern is their fighter jets and their ability to control the air.

"We were surprised by their speed and stealth abilities. We were caught off guard by these aircraft. We will not have the same disadvantage in our next attack. We should have known they would have brought their ramjet technology to their fighters, but we didn't think they had the time to make that happen. Neither our satellites nor spy flights over their research complex picked this up. We also should have known they would have the best technology since they have been supplying these advancements to other countries and the UN for a couple of years through Texas Instruments. They have apparently developed the next generation of stealth-cloaking skins, which are undetectable to our systems. The good news is that we were able to see them at the beginning of the confrontation and when they went into ramjet mode due to the heat generated on the skins. But our algorithms were confused by the speeds.

"We do believe we can fight them with some of our most advanced fighters, and we have a couple of other strategies to beat them. Their ramjets can only fire for one to two minutes, so we believe we can attack them after they return to conventional power. If that is the case, we need to spread our fighters at the ends of their runs and between their targets as they return to Texas. Our engineers believe we can get a targeting signature off the planes during their acceleration and then determine where they should end up after they run out of burn. Even though we know we will take casualties as they are in the attack, we believe we can beat them with our overwhelming number of conventional fighters. If we can take out these aircraft one at a time until they are gone, we will then take control of the skies, which will be the end of their protection overhead. After that, it will be simply a few attacks on their infrastructure before they realize surrender will be their only option."

Admiral Romelov spoke up next. "Madame Secretary, we have looked at all the data we were able to retrieve from the attack, and we have some encouraging news from the air battle. When we initially detected the enemy aircraft, we were able to document some engine signatures as well as defeat some of their stealth technologies. Our technicians are working on their coding now. We believe we can solve their advantage in a week or less. We believe we can overwhelm them with our pure numbers of ships and aircraft to begin to eliminate their air force.

"We also think we should use our advantage in cruise missiles from long range to take out some of their strategic targets. We can position our ships a thousand miles off their coast and launch a barrage of missiles that can fly through their laser defenses. Many will be destroyed, but enough will get through using different codes to get to their targets. We need to focus on Bush Air Force Base and destroy it to eliminate their ability to get their jets in the air. If we have a coordinated attack with thousands of missiles, enough of them will get to their destinations to send a message. This will not only cripple them and their efforts to fight us but will also buy us some time to defeat their technological advantages. We will overwhelm them with our sheer numbers."

Secretary Polentas replied, "I am not sure you men understand the seriousness of this attack. We do need to have a decisive and immediate counterattack to maintain our strength over the rest of the world. Right now, our member nations are discouraged and not sure if we can defeat Texas. We must make a statement, which means these attacks must be successful and decisive. If not, then you will need to use a more aggressive solution to cause the maximum amount of damage to force them to rethink this war."

Captain Thomas was leading his squadron, checking the waterfront facilities of the Gulf. They were on maximum alert while every precaution was being taken. They knew they were now targets, so they were staying well within the Texas International waters even though Texas claimed half of the Gulf. Their primary mission was locating and detecting enemy aircraft coming from South American or Mexican bases. Nothing had been detected, although that did not mean there was nothing out there. The UN had more advanced stealth technology, as they found out weeks ago.

Their secondary mission was testing their ground-based anti-aircraft batteries. They crisscrossed the batteries at different altitudes, stealth codes, and speeds to try to defeat their ability to track as they prepared for the potential attacks. This was exhausting and monotonous, but they knew they had been compromised in the past, and it only takes one to get through, and thousands could be killed. The drills went on for hours and hours as their bodies began to mold into their seats like a catcher's mitt in late innings when the radio broke, "Rattler, we have detected unidentified aircraft nine hundred miles south of Houston and need you to get a better reading. It's on a north-northeast track, and I need to see if you can ID it."

"Roger that. Send me your coordinates, frequencies, and programming codes to locate."

"Firefly, this is Rattler. We have hostiles approaching south of us nine hundred miles south southeast; we need to ID. Take your squadron to the east of his position, and we'll fly to the west to try to get a reading and triangulate. Be careful; this could be a trap. Let us know if you get any reading on him. You will be getting coordinates and codes momentarily."

"Roger that."

Thomas and his squadron rolled east with their cloaking on max spectrum while they scanned the horizon, looking for any breaks in the bogie's stealth software. They traveled halfway when their displays started showing blinks across their screens. It looked like there was some type of software malfunction with dots blinking on and off across the heads-up monitor as well as the three-dimension positioning display with dots looking like the stars of the entire solar system.

He spoke to his right wing, "Coyote, I'm having software problems with my Laze-lume display. There seems to be a lack of stability and getting random reflections covering my screen. What are you seeing?"

"That is an affirmative, Rattler. My screen is acting up and looks like a night sky blinking off and on. Either my software is off and needs a reset or—"

Just as he said—there were laser detections from every direction. The 3D-illuminator looked like water fountains as streams of red were coming from every direction and raining down on his squadron like an inverted fire hose. He watched as three of his squad jets exploded while he screamed into his helmet, "It's an ambush! All fighters hit your Ram with maximum deflections and go up to a hundred thousand—*now!*"

Rattler hit the ramjet shooting him to Mach 9 as he began taking out bandits ten at a time. His counter was over a hundred shot down as he saw an explosion. Thomas hit the ramjet shooting him to Mach 9 as he began taking out bandits flying next to him, knowing it was one of his squadron having a midair collision, unable to fly through the gauntlet of enemy fighters. Once he got up to the ceiling and out of their range, he had the advantage; he called into his mike, "Firefly, are you still there?"

"Roger that, Rat, we took some hits and lost two and one limping back. What are your orders?"

"Move your squad east, and we will veer yours for a pincer attack, then refire your Rams and fight our way back to the base. There must be over five thousand aircraft up here. Let's do this!"

"Careful, boys, by our ground estimates, there are over five thousand fighters up there and are coming out of your south like a dark cloud of locust. You need to get up above them and work your way back to base. Try to stay above them if you can. We are scrambling everything we have, and you should have help in a few minutes. Godspeed!"

He slammed back in his seat once more as he and his intuitive fire computers were hitting enemy after enemy while they weaved above the swarms of jets back to the Texas coast. He had never seen this many fighters in one place, even when he was doing international maneuvers with the US Air Force. Once he leveled off at fifty thousand, he hit the ramjet one more time as he saw a flash of another one of his aircraft exploding. He was hit repeatedly but never with enough energy to destroy his deflectors. Lasers were hitting his deflection skin from every direction constantly, and it was doing exactly what it was made to do. He could see the mass of fighters following him like a speeding cloud of death toward the Houston refineries, which could only mean one thing.

"Base, this is Rattler. You need to scramble all your jets and have a refuel team ready for me as I need to do a rolling refuel. You need a crash team for some damaged aircraft you have coming in with me. We have over a thousand aircraft heading toward the south coast area, and we need to get as many birds up as fast as we can."

"Listen, squadron, any planes with major damage, land first but get to the fire rescue zones as fast as possible since any planes that can fly need to get back up here with more fuel. Keep the tankers on the ground since they would be target practice up here. Anyone with nonthreatening damage needing repairs stay up until we can get the rotation done and back up. Okay, those needing to get down, land now."

Rattler and Firefly's squadrons made the turnaround in ten minutes with fresh fuel and recharging the deflectors. They were up with every fighter Texas had, which was currently around three hundred. They headed straight south to join the dogfights going on over the Houston refineries. They could see the smoke coming from the fires, which covered dozens of square miles.

Thomas's monitors were lit up from horizon to horizon with targets. He had streaked back up to a hundred thousand to begin his attack dive through the hundreds of fighters on his screen. Hitting the ramjet, he targeted for his computers to hit targets dozens at a time with the counter over three hundred kills. It seemed like there was no end to the number of dots — just like there was no end to the lasers hitting his plane. As he negotiated between the explosions, he heard distress calls from his fighters as their planes were getting knocked down one after another.

His warning light on his deflectors lit up, which told him they were about to fail, forcing him back to the base. He had already logged over three hundred fifty kills and hit the ramjet one last time to get out of the fray. As he turned, he noticed the remaining bandits were turning to the south and heading back. He wasn't sure if they were out of fuel or aircraft, but in his mind, he didn't care. He was just hoping the fight was over as he was bone tired and needed some rest.

Just as he thought about rolling back to the barn, he noticed a spark on his left flap. In a flash, his panel went black, and a laser ripped across his wing, cutting it from the fuselage. The plane immediately went into a twelve hundred miles per hour death spin, hurtling toward the Gulf. The centrifugal force had his hands pinned to the sides of the plane without enough strength to reach down for the ejector lever as the ocean surface came racing at his face.

"Eject, eject, eject, 452, eject!"

The church hall was filled with men and women full of anticipation as the chatter grew louder among their families. The church had been transformed into a dining hall so tables could be spread around for the potluck and celebration. The families were dressed in their Sunday best, although living in the woods for six months or a year did not exactly make for the finery of a New Year's ball in the city. That did not put a damper on the festivities as the band played, and a choir sang some old-time gospels raising spirits of the entire compound.

Pastor David, Steven, and June walked in from the side of the stage, pushing the Texas Ranger in a wheelchair. He looked gaunt and weak. He had obviously been beaten severely, requiring a cast on his left leg, and his fingers were wrapped where his fingernails were torn out. His face was swollen and bruised, and he had a black eye and numerous cuts on the side of his face and arms. The crowd erupted as he looked out over them and slowly lifted his hand to wave and give the thumbs-up sign. He smiled at them through broken and missing teeth as the entire hall began singing "Amazing Grace." As the song went higher, the tears flowed faster, and it continued to grow louder and louder. The hall rang with power and hope. When it ended, the silence was deafening as they stood in silence, anticipating the Texas Ranger's words.

Steven rolled him forward then handed Ranger the microphone; the ovation grew and grew as the members responded with the love they were feeling for his return. "Thank you so much, brothers and sisters! God is so good, and He has been giving me my strength back every day since the rescue. It was a miracle you found me and even more that you were able to get into that prison and break me out. Your timing was amazing.

"After they caught us in the ambush down in the city, they took me to the UN compound and beat me for hours to get the names and addresses of our members. They kept me there for two days and beat me every six hours for two hours at a time until they moved me up to the prison. I was supposed to be killed immediately, but they thought they could get the names and locations out of me since we were a big thorn in their side. They would beat me one day, let me heal a bit the next, and then beat me again the entire time I was there. They offered me all sorts of enticements and temptations if I would just give them a few names or locations of our safe houses, but God gave me the strength to endure it one more day. I just tried to remember what my Savior went through for me, and the beatings did not compare.

"I was driving them crazy since I never broke and was always in a joyous mood, singing and praising God throughout the ordeal. They could not understand why I wasn't bitter, angry, or complaining but continued to give God the glory, recite scripture, and sing gospels. I was able to share the gospel with two of my guards, and they eventually came to Christ, which filled my heart with even more joy beyond their comprehension. They never could understand why I wouldn't break but just kept singing and praising God.

"The warden realized I wasn't going to give them any names or information, so I was scheduled to go to the death chamber the next day—then God rescued me. Thousands of men went to that death ward, and none of them ever returned, so I was sure they were going to kill me. I was ready. I knew the Lord Jesus Christ had given me a life I could only dream of and was ready and praying for His will to be done. I was praying daily this movement would continue to sustain and grow stronger. I prayed for all of your health and protection, and you rescued me, praise God."

A huge roar went up as the people jumped to their feet, praising God for his safety.

"When I saw Steven's hover jet lights landing and heard the gunfire, I knew God was saving me from my death, and then when I saw Steven, I knew God was truly in control. He is in control of this entire war, and He has told me to take our battle back to New York and go to the center of this battle. We are to attack and take out the United Nations compound. While they are focused on Texas and defeating them, they will not be looking for an attack on the compound, which is exactly why we need to go there.

"You must know, on paper, this looks like a suicide mission, but as we say, 'One man with God is an unbeatable army.' We must have faith in Him, and we will have the advantages of surprise as well as knowing the area better than our enemies do. We have built a network through the subways, which will allow us back into the city without detection. We know the gaps in the security and can get a strong force into the compound area and can develop a plan to accomplish our mission of taking down the Secretariat Tower.

"With that, I want to thank you for all your prayers, which helped sustain me through some dark times, and it's now time to celebrate. Those dark times, however, were the times I felt closest to God, and that's had a purging effect on me. During one of the beatings, I remember feeling I was going to die, and the Holy Spirit spoke to me to keep hanging on and stay strong since God had a plan for me. He told me to dig in and give more of my life to Him. Then the pain simply disappeared, and it's as if I was no longer in my body, and the torture never was effective. It was like a cleansing fire bringing me to a higher level of faith. So, brothers and sisters, let's celebrate God's mercy on all of us and begin to take our faith to the next level and truly live our lives by faith."

As the band struck up, they could hear a low rumble building in the distance. It was the sound everyone in the hall knew and feared. Outside they could hear the anti-aircraft batteries going off and those batteries taking incoming laser and missile fire. The hall lights began flashing, letting everyone know they were under attack. As the women and children headed for the basement, the men grabbed their Kevlar deflector gear and weapons then headed for their battle stations outside.

When they ran from the building, their worst fears were realized. A giant Hover Fortress was over the middle of the compound with UN troops repelling down ropes to the ground in full battle gear. Loudspeakers were blaring for the people to surrender as they were surrounded and overpowered. The men were firing from their fortified positions, but the troopers were wearing deflection Kevlar, making their weapons less than effective. They were able to make some concentration hits, knocking a couple of troopers to the ground, but the Hover Fortress over their heads kept them pinned down with no way of escape.

The Fortress was firing from position to position, taking out the defenders without any real effect from the anti-aircraft batteries. Either they were already taken out, or the fighters were not wanting to be detected until they had an open missile strike, which would mean certain death in return. The compound looked like a raging forest fire rather than the peaceful compound it had been a few minutes earlier.

Steven looked over at Ranger and said, "I'm taking up the Black Stallion to fight that thing. It is the only chance we have."

Ranger looked at him. "Do you really think you can stop that Fortress?"

"I don't know how I can, but like you said, 'One man with God is an unbeatable army.' I have to try."

June looked at him and added, "You can do this, honey. They are depending on you. We will be praying for you, and God will help you find a way." She knew there was a good chance he would not be coming back, but he was their only chance of stopping the Hover Fortress.

As Steven sprinted for the Black Stallion with laser blasts hitting all around him, Pastor David and June began to take Ranger downstairs when he objected, "I am not going to hide down in the basement. Take me to the second-level balcony so I can watch the battle. Let's go!"

They pushed him up to the balcony where he could see the lasers and missiles flying in every direction, lighting the evening in a crisscrossing maze of lasers. It was a spectacular light show and deadly at the same time.

Outside there was mass confusion as the troopers were working their way toward the main hall. Steven dashed around one of the cabins and looked across the meadow where the Stallion was hidden. He pushed his emergency remote, and the Stallion fired up and shot across the meadow where he could jump in the cockpit. He shot straight up, and banking around, he could not believe the massiveness of this fortress. It had to be more than a full city block across and had no visible weakness. His only thought was to somehow hit the intakes if it were possible.

He dove straight down behind it, hoping he could remain invisible for a few seconds, which he apparently was, unless it was setting him up for a trap. His screen was showing search detectors hitting his skin, but nothing was marking him. He crept up over the top and looked down at the massive blades spinning below the huge air intakes. He could feel the swirling tornado of wind buffeting the Stallion as he attempted to get close enough for a shot when a downdraft pulled the Stallion into the intake blades. This was worse than landing on a derrick in a raging hurricane on the Gulf. Hitting his full reverse power, he attempted to pull away from the instant death staring at him in the enormous whirling blades.

He was two feet from the intake with the Black Stallion fighting with everything it had to stay out of the thundering eggbeaters. The powerful winds were rocking and shaking the craft in a violent fight for survival as he fought the controls with every fiber of his being. He felt this instant was his only brief chance before becoming sliced into a million pieces and pulled the trigger. The laser cut the blades with surprising ease as the titanium shrapnel went screaming through the massive hulk tearing electronics and aircraft as the metal parts flying at ten thousand r.p.m. did their mortal damage to the giant beast. One superheated shard shot through the fuel tanks, starting an initial explosion, illuminating the entire compound, igniting secondary and tertiary explosions. These explosions sent fireballs into the sky, throwing the Black Stallion back over a hundred and fifty yards while Steven fought the controls as his Black Stallion cartwheeled through the air out of control and eventually landed on the top of an ancient oak tree.

The massive hull of the hover rocked right and then left before it suddenly fell out of the sky and into the ground, causing a final immense fireball while the stormtroopers looked on in stunned disbelief. A cheer went up from the compound defenders as they made a final charge at the

The Republic of Texas

enemy troopers who were dropping their weapons and raised their hands in shocked surrender.

Steven shook his head, trying to get his bearings and figure out where he was. Once he did, he chuckled at how he ended up in a tree. After he caught his breath, he restarted the Stallion and limped it back to the church while the entire compound erupted in cheers, pulling him out of the cockpit.

June met him with tears running down her cheeks. "I knew you could do it. I knew God would protect you, and I love you so much."

THE EYE OF THE STORM

The Texas Security Council met three floors under the capitol building in a reinforced bunker, which was built shortly after Texas declared its sovereignty from the United States against the chance of war. The commanders of all the armed forces were in the room with President Stewart, Vice President Chapman, Senator Jackson, and Jeff Drake representing Moses Enterprises, along with leaders of the other strategic industries.

President Stewart spoke first, "Ladies and gentlemen, we are at a critical stage, and we are in a difficult situation with our fighter aircraft. We are down to eighty-five combat-ready fighters, and if we have another attack like we had today, we will be defenseless to their attacks by noon tomorrow. This would make our skies empty of our fighters so they could attack our industries unopposed. Barring a miracle, we must seriously consider our options—including our surrender."

Senator Jackson burst out, "There is no surrender in Texas! Our history began at the Alamo against impossible odds, where we fought to the last man. Texans will fight to their last heartbeat, and I swear I will fight until my last breath on this earth as a free Texan!"

A cheer rose and echoed off the mahogany-paneled walls of the bunker.

"That was all I wanted to hear and exactly the way I hoped you would react. I don't know how we can fight this war against these overwhelming odds of the pure might and numbers of the world against us. We need a miracle to save us and our great country from its demise. General Thompson, can you update us on our situation in both aircraft and land-based laser systems."

"Thank you, Mr. President. As you stated earlier, we are down to eighty-five fully operational aircraft with another five to ten which can be repaired by morning. Every able-bodied mechanic and pilot has volunteered to help, and they are working as hard as they can around the clock. We cannot survive another attack like today, but we can hopefully withstand another two days if all goes well.

"Our land-based lasers are in good shape, and we should be able to stop any low-flying stealth missile attacks as well as conventional warheads. However, subspace and space-based missiles are in a directed free fall and will hit close to whatever they are programmed to hit. In addition, high-altitude bombers are outside of the effective range of our lasers and would avoid a downing hit, especially with their newly advanced deflectors. Our fighters that can get in at close range are the only effective weapon against a fully-stealth armored aircraft."

President Stewart asked, "General Martinez, can you give us an update on any technology and weapons development which we may not be aware of?"

"Well, President Stewart, I wish I had something in hand, but we are advancing on improving the distance of our lasers as well as improving our stealth technology. Our techs have been working overtime for the past three months. That's why we were able to have the successes we saw today. Our main issue is the time and expense of producing more fighters. We don't have the capabilities or resources of the entire world combined.

"Tomorrow, we're going to launch our newest weapon into the war—which is a ramjet drone fighter. We've been flying messenger drones around the world at supersonic speeds for quite some time, although they've been limited by power and payload. To incorporate our weaponry into these drones, we must power the lasers and cloaking. We've had to miniaturize power generators beyond technologies we've used in the past. We've installed a ramjet booster into the propulsion system. There is nothing that can match the speed. Their maneuverability is the question. Our engineers have been coordinating from every industry to make these aircraft weapon systems work. We've had some breakthroughs in the past two weeks and have been testing our initial prototypes, which we'll take into combat tomorrow. We're going to test fly twenty-five, but

The Republic of Texas

if they work, we can bring on over two hundred per day, which can buy us some more time.

"We don't know how effective they will be since they've only been tested in our labs with simulated test flights to recreate dogfights. But to put them in actual combat situations is anybody's guess. We do believe we have some pretty good remote pilots who've been flying these for years; however, how they're going to react and avoid detection in combat is the question. They've never shot at live aircraft or been shot at live before. If they are marginally effective, we can buy some time and defend against these overwhelming odds. If not, we will have to improve their designs and weapons until we can have a working drone fighter."

Jeff Drake spoke up, "If these drones work, we will provide any funding and engineers you may need to produce five hundred per day. I've spoken with Steven Moses, and he has directed me to put his company's entire resources at the disposal of the war effort. If there is anything you need, simply say the word, and we'll try to provide it."

All the industry leaders confirmed their support for the effort.

President Stewart responded, "I expect these drones will do the job very well. They have been the best craft in the world, so it really comes down to the weapons systems, which it appears you have perfected or are close to perfection. We'll see tomorrow. In any event, we have no real options, so we would like to set a goal of producing five hundred per day. Is that possible? If we can, it would offset their advantages in a few days and would overwhelm them in weeks."

General Martinez answered, "I suppose we can attempt to make that happen, but we really don't have the space or facilities to manufacture at that level. We would need some help from other industries. Texas Aircraft could help us if we sent them the schematics and programs to manufacture these drones and weapons. Is that possible?"

Drake answered, "I'll talk with Davis Thompson, our CEO, tonight. We *will* make this happen, and it's possible that Texas Hovercraft may take some of the manufacturing to help produce these drones. It would take some modification and engineering design work, but they should be able to produce them, too. We'll get our engineers over there working tonight to make this happen."

President Stewart finished the meeting. "Gentlemen, this may be the weapon we have been needing to even things up against their overwhelming numbers. Nobody is sleeping tonight and perhaps tomorrow, so let's give this push everything we have. Our people are counting on us."

The pilots' meeting had been going on an hour when Rattler walked in, shocking everyone. He was hobbling and favoring his right leg with his arm in a sling and looked like he had been in a fight with a mountain lion, but his smile was still there, as was the familiar sparkle in his eyes. The room erupted in cheers as he waved and walked to the front and looked out over the pilots.

His squad wingman, Firefly, looked shocked. "How in the world did you survive that hit? I saw you get blasted by at least twenty lasers taking your wing off and then death spin into the ocean at over Mach 6 and no chute?"

"You're right; it was a miracle! I was hit by a multi-focused shot that sheared off my wing. I was in a spin that plastered me into my seat, completely immobile with the centrifugal force holding me fast. I thought I was a goner. If not for the audio backup ejection pod, there would have been no way to survive. I barely got out the fourth eject vocal command before I passed out, and the plane splashed then exploded. Even though I must have ejected, I hit the water so hard it felt like a parking lot as the retro rockets barely had time to fire, let alone make for any controlled landing. The plane must have been at just the right angle for me to not be pancaked.

"I was knocked out cold by the impact, and thankfully the rescue crews were on scene in short order to save me from the pod capsizing and drowning. The long and short of it, I used another of my nine lives in that crash. I should be dead right now. But thank God, I am still alive and ready to fight more than ever. Just a little bruised and stiff all over. Hopefully, we have a replacement fighter for me to get back up tomorrow and get more UN bogies. I look much worse than I feel. The good news is, I am meeting a lot of nurses with these trips to the hospital. Who knows—one more crash, and I may be married!" The room broke up in laughter.

Commander Jackson responded to his request, "Squad Leader Thomas, make sure to get yourself checked out. Some of the soft tissue damage won't show up until tomorrow morning, but if everything checks out, I'm sure we can find an extra aircraft for you to go up and shoot down more bad guys. Thank you for the job you've been doing, Thomas. You're leading the Air Force in confirmed kills at 487, with today's total alone at 239. Congratulations."

The room erupted in applause as his fellow pilots gave him a standing ovation while chanting, "Rattler! Rattler! Rattler!"

Commander Jackson interrupted the celebration. "Gentlemen, let's get back to the business at hand. We expect another massive attack in the morning. The UN must believe we are out of fighters—which we are. We are down to eighty-five functional aircraft. This means we will have only half the fighters we have pilots to fly. Which brings me to the second part of this meeting.

"We have a new weapon being rolled out in the morning, which is a fighter drone with ramjet boosters. This is an upgrade of the shuttle drones we've been using for high-speed courier deliveries around the world. These drones were fast and nimble, to begin with, but they have been completely reworked to turn them into a potential equalizer since they can produce these drones in the hundreds rather than the dozens of fighters they make now.

"That said, we need to have the pilots who do not have a fighter and can fly some of these aircraft while training the techs who are test flying them now. It will be like being in a simulator without all the hydraulic movement. The visuals will be shone inside three-hundred-sixty-degree visual goggles for your intuitive targeting and defense systems. You will have the same electronics and displays you have in your fighter, and all the weapons systems will feel the same. I really think these drones can become the difference makers in the war. With all of that, who will volunteer to fly these drones rather than you fighters?"

Terry Thomas slowly got up out of his seat. "I will volunteer to fly a drone, Commander. I may be a bit stiff in the morning, but this sounds like a new challenge and where I can be the most effective."

"Thanks, Thomas. How about you be the Wing Commander down at Johnson Space, where they will be controlling these new drones. Who else would like to volunteer?"

Pilots stood up around the room as they lined up to do their part and stay in the fight.

The main clearing of the compound was covered by the wreckage of the Hover Fortress. They had recovered twenty-nine bodies from the airship and found three still alive who were in the infirmary recovering. The massive size of the craft was incredible. Even after the explosions and fires had consumed much of the fuselage, it still covered two football fields. The fact it landed in the middle of the clearing away from the compound log buildings was the most stunning miracle of all.

It was ten-thirty in the morning, so the men stopped the weapons salvage and clearing of the wreckage and began walking over to the main chapel where the strategy meeting was being called for the next four hours before they began packing and leaving. There had been a large increase in the number of people inside the compound over the past couple of days as word of their victory had spread among the church groups.

Ranger was wheeled up to the podium and began speaking to the overflow crowd. "It's time to take the fight directly to the United Nations compound. God is with us and showing His glory. He will now finish revealing His power. Over the last year, my leaders and I have been designing ways to defeat many of their defenses, and now we have faith in the plan that we believe will work.

"We all know they are being distracted by the war effort, and there is no way they are expecting an attack on New York. One of the benefits of being hunted by them for all these years is we know how to get in out of the city without being detected. We know all their defenses, detection locations, and techniques as well as how to defeat them. We're going to need to get over a thousand men into their compound area to fully engage their security forces. While they're engaged with you, we will be bringing in the real strike with Steven Moses's hover jet.

"These men, with the aid of some of our armored trucks, are going to mount an attack from the south to draw all the fire from the compound in their direction as well as their troops and hovers to defeat this attack. This should leave the northern sector of the compound open for the real attack.

"Steven, are you ready for one more mission with the Black Stallion?"

Steven looked up and replied, "Of course, I'm ready if it will help end this war, but I don't think the hover can go since it was pretty damaged in this last skirmish. It's not very stable, and the crash knocked out my stealth computers. We can attempt a remote download for upgraded software to see if that will help, but any way you slice it, getting close enough to the UN building for a kill shot is suicide. I just don't know how I can get in past all of the security."

"Leave that to us, Steven. There's more than one way to skin a cat, and in this case, we will get you in. I will be flying shotgun and can show you the way in without them seeing you. We will have to fit the Stallion with stronger lasers and install some launchers that we have, which can deliver enough payload to level the building."

Steven replied, "You mean you want me to destroy the entire building and everyone in it? I don't know if that's the right way to fight."

"Steven, I understand what you're saying, but you kill a snake by cutting off its head. The United Nations building is their head. They declared war on Texas, and you know they were trying to take us out with the attack two days ago. We're going to do to them what they tried to do to us and, God willing, will put an end to the UN and this war!"

The building erupted in cheers.

"Okay, let's divide into our groups and go over the details. After the meeting with your leaders, we will be loading the men who are going to be on the ground, so do your packing and be ready to leave at twenty-thirty hours tonight. We have to do this right since we only will have one opportunity to surprise them."

The city was quiet, and Secretary-General Polentas could see for miles across the light-speckled horizon. There were more swaths of black, but there was still beauty in the night. She could see nearly sixty miles of the Atlantic shoreline from her office. She thought of how the people in all those houses were sleeping peacefully while she and her team were spending most of the night preparing their war designs.

It was nearing midnight, and she was a bit annoyed but curious why Ambassador Herrmoza had called an emergency meeting with just her. She had an idea about why but decided to let him explain what he was there for.

"Madame Secretary, thank you for your time. I have been speaking with our Air Force generals, and we have a very troubling development beginning to materialize. Our pilots are refusing to go up and attack the Texan ramjets. They are afraid of the numbers that are being shot down, and even though they know they are close to finishing the job of defeating Texas from the air, they don't like their odds of who will be coming back.

"Unless we defeat them decisively tomorrow, we may not have many pilots who will attack the next day. We need to do something powerful and dramatic to force them to the negotiating table for surrender—and that is a nuclear attack on Dallas."

Secretary Polentas replied, "I gave my word to the generals we would wait until tomorrow to decide on whether we would use nuclear weapons or not."

"I understand, but things have changed. I have spoken to Admiral Romelov and Air Force General Davis. They both agree we really don't have the time to wait if we cannot defeat them tomorrow. We must use everything at our disposal and do it while we have a window of opportunity for victory. You have the authority to call an attack during a time of war and deploy any weapons you deem necessary."

"Thank you, Ambassador Herrmoza. The wholesale killing of upward of two million people or more is not something I can decide like this in the middle of the night. I will call an emergency meeting in the morning, and we can discuss and decide this at that time."

THE FINAL FURY

The sun was just rising over East Texas as the flight crews readied the flight lines for battle. The pilots fired their jets as they pointed their birds into the golden rising sun. They headed south over the deep blue Gulf, expecting an attack from all directions; however, it was surprisingly quiet this morning. It was as if they were flying routine patrol before the war began, except they all knew the war was here. The only noticeable difference was the lack of shipping and the smoke billowing from the refineries surrounding Houston.

Firefly looked over at his wingman. "Titan, be on your toes. This feels like the calm before the storm, and we have a Category 5 hurricane coming straight at us. We are severely outnumbered and outgunned, which means we have them right where God wants them. They want today to be the final battle of the war, and we must make sure that doesn't happen. Say your prayers and be ready to fight like you're at the Alamo, and this is Texas' last stand."

As soon as he finished the statement, his display Christmas-treed like it had never lit up before. Next, the air ignited with laser tracers bouncing from every direction as the Texans fired their ramjets and climbed to a hundred thousand feet, escaping the red glowing spiderwebs of death. While they climbed and watched as the earth faded below, they cut the Gulf into sectors while they accounted for the hundreds of aircraft they were about to attack.

As Firefly pointed his squadron down into his quadrant of bogies, he screamed into his mask, "Y'all don't mess with Texas, ya hear?"

Firefly felt an edgy calm come over himself as he suddenly became a part of the jet as much as a wing or a rudder, understanding how the plane reacted before he touched the stick. He was hitting everything he saw while looking at his 3D interior display light up with mini-explosions sparkling in every direction, giving the cockpit a celestial look. His kill counter seemed to be rolling like a slot machine, quickly passing a hundred, and he had only been up for twenty minutes when he looked to go for more fuel and a recharge. When he rolled back toward Bush Air Force Base field, he was hit by a multiple burst, making a surge in his defensive software, causing it to fail, momentarily exposing his aircraft to all the enemy fire. In a split second, it was enveloped by lasers from every direction as his jet exploded instantaneously.

Terry Thomas had been familiarizing himself with the controls of the drones for the last four hours. It had many of the same motions; however, they were more responsive with a much tighter turning response than the trainers. They seemed to dart like jackrabbits rather than bank and climb like a jet. This was something new, something he only dreamed his planes could do without the mass and controlled velocity. He now sat in the actual control seat and slid on the flight goggles as he gave the drone flaps and engine a once-over before he taxied onto the runway. He had never been this nervous since his first training flight in the Navy, feeling anxious anticipation in his gut.

"Squadron, prepare for takeoff. Okay, hit the burners, and let's go into the Texas blue yonder."

The actual feel of the plane was nonexistent, which meant he had to adjust to not flying by feel, but on the other hand, he could dart without any concern for G-force or the muscle fatigue that goes with it. His goggles lit up with targets as he entered the kill zone and ordered into his microphone, "Hit the Rams and let's get above this battle. Techs, could you lay out some quadrants for us when we get up to a hundred thousand?"

When they were up to altitude, he gave the order, "Okay, boys, point them to the deck, and let's go see what these birds can do."

He made his maiden dive while hitting targets with his intuitive targeting. It had the same power in weapons, if not a bit stronger, and the

The Republic of Texas

banking ability was very surprising at the speeds his plane was flying. The flight computers kept the plane stable even when he tended to over-correct as he tried to match what he was seeing with his lack of feel. The size of his plane made it even harder for bad guys to detect as the power and quickness made for a deadly combination. He made numerous runs on his targets, making the kill counter spin like an old-fashioned gas pump. Thinking of which, his fuel tanks showed they better get back on the ground as he called out, "Let's get our drones back on the deck and refuel. I don't know about the rest of you, but this fighter is as good as any craft I have flown."

The battle that day was as fierce as any they had ever experienced. As the sun was setting, they had lost only thirty fighters and two drones. The losses for the United Nations were well over eleven hundred fighters. As Terry turned his drone back to base for the last time, he took one more ramjet booster up to a hundred thousand when his monitor showed a giant flash from the north. He could see the flash coming in his direction and then hit his drone, knocking it backward as a monstrous electrical pulse hit his electronics.

Once he began to regain control of his craft, he rolled in the direction he saw the flash, and within seconds, he saw the massive mushroom clouds rising above Dallas.

Ranger burst into the prayer room where Steven and June were in prayer, "They destroyed Dallas with a nuclear attack last night! The news is reporting there is nothing living for a fifty-mile radius. There must be millions of dead, and who knows how many injured. This is the worst attack in history, and we have no idea how many more nuclear warheads they have aimed at Texas. We need success in our attack today."

June was crying as they lifted their heads, and she began to take the ring off her finger. "Steven, this is an impossible mission, but you have to try it to end this war, and I'm so afraid you may not be coming back.

I want you to wear my ring as a memory of both Sandy and me, to help carry you back to us. I love you more than I have ever loved anyone and want to marry you and give you a house full of screaming children, but this is bigger than any of that. Take my ring as a symbol of both of our hearts. While the world seems like it is falling apart, we will be kneeling on your heart in prayer. Perhaps our ring will heal the wound aching in your chest from her death. So, I will be praying that Sandy is still looking down from the hands of Jesus to watch over you. All the women will be here praying a hedge of protection over both of you."

Steven was touched, "I do not deserve either of you women, let alone both. This ring is the greatest gift anyone has ever given me. I can't guarantee the pain of Sandy's death will ever go away, but I am so blessed to have a woman who understands my wound. I can never thank God enough for bringing you into my life. You know I will be coming back to hold you to that promise of a house full of kids."

June blushed through cheeks covered with tears as she gave him a wet kiss goodbye and hugged Ranger. "I have never been so proud of anyone in my life. You two are the bravest men I know."

Walking into the shed, Steven nodded to the mechanic as he looked up from his diagnostics readying the Black Stallion. "Brady, have you been able to download the repairs from Texas for my stealth software?"

"Yeah, we were able to repair most of it, as well as install a new upgrade they just developed; however, there are a couple of glitches you picked up in the crash that I wasn't really able to fix. Your hardware took a big hit when you crashed into the tree. You will be visible to certain frequencies, and there will be flashes of the software just stopping for a reboot, so be on your toes. They may have some looks at you when it has software conflicts. This will be especially dangerous when you get in range of the compound as they have the most sophisticated detection outside of Texas. You may be invisible or visible; I just can't tell what will happen. It simply has some code in it which was corrupted into something I and the guys in Texas have never seen before, so it's anybody's guess how it will respond under attack. This is going to be a risky mission, Mr. Moses."

"Thanks, Brady; I know you did everything you could. Say a prayer for the Black Stallion."

"I will, and Godspeed."

Secretary Polentas sat in the war room on the twenty-fourth floor of the Secretariat Tower with her top military generals who were directing the war. It was a crystal-clear morning, although there was a feeling of defeat in the room as they were not able to eliminate the last of the fighters the day before.

Secretary Polentas opened, "I understand the consequences of yesterday's defeat, but what I want to know is what we can do in the future to turn this war around to our advantage. We may have to change our strategy if we are going to defeat the Texans. General Davis, can you and Admiral Romelov give us a rundown on where we are from the Air Force's perspective?"

"Yes, Madame Secretary. We have analyzed our losses overnight, and it does not look good. We lost over twelve hundred jet fighters and brought down only twelve Texan jets as well as only two of their new fighter drones. We are completely outgunned from a technological standpoint. We are not able to defeat their software or breakthrough it unless they have a software glitch that reveals them to our LASAR detection.

"The other side of the coin is they have broken our codes, and our stealth software is ineffective against them. They can target our aircraft in multiple targeting sequences making our fighters easy pickings. Now we must battle their new ramjet drones, which are even harder to find, faster, and more maneuverable than their fighters. By all measures, they have air superiority over Texas and the gulf."

Admiral Romelov added, "Madame Secretary, I have to agree with everything General Davis just reported, and it has caused a serious demoralizing effect on our pilots. They know the odds are stacked against them and have no trust in their aircraft when they go up. Add the fact we have lost most of our best fighter pilots, and we are in a situation we have the least experienced pilots flying older and less advanced aircraft going against the most advanced aircraft in the world. And it's getting worse by the day. We cannot simply overwhelm them with our numbers since we cannot pierce their defensive weaponry."

"Ambassador Herrmoza, do you have anything to add?"

"Yes, Madame Secretary. We are in a difficult position, although not as impossible as the generals are making it out to be. We really have two choices. Since we do not have air superiority, we have no way of destroying enough of their aircraft to force them to accept the resolution. So, then we either negotiate a surrender agreement or send a message that wars have consequences. We only have one advantage they do not have, which is our nuclear arsenal."

General Davis spoke up, "There is no way we can make this a nuclear war. It was bad enough you two decided to launch an attack on Dallas against my demands, but I am not going to agree to a nuclear war on Texas. They were part of the United States, and my country will not tolerate you destroying one of our fellow states. There is still a kinship between us and Texas, and the attack has Americans in shock."

Secretary-General Polentas broke in, "Gentlemen, we are not going to decide right now whether we are going to escalate this into a nuclear war. It is true we have two choices, either negotiate a surrender or use the nuclear option. We will meet back here at noon and discuss our options."

Instantly the alarms in the building began howling, and the generals' phones started ringing when General Sanchez came barging into the room with a look of concern, "Secretary-General, there is an attack on the compound coming up First Avenue from the south. It looks like a well-organized militia with over a thousand men."

Steven and Ranger had been hugging the earth under the power lines to avoid detection over the past two hours. The electron leakage of the antiquated power lines made a perfect electron field to avoid satellite detection. There were no people around as these lines took the roughest mountain paths and had been off-limits for the past five years from wheeled traffic, making a route for them to be unseen from the normal traffic, allowing them to save computer power. They slowed to a hover as they approached New York City at Woodlawn Station on the Green Line, waiting for the 9:15 to pull out as they watched from a thousand feet away.

Ranger instructed Steven, "Now you are going to have to get right in behind the train as it enters the subway. There is an invisible envelope that extends ten feet behind the train that is a dead spot in their detection system. The electric motors cause too much static electricity for the sensors to see through. They never expected people to be there, so they never picked up on the gap in their system, which is how we have smuggled people, guns, and Bibles into the Burroughs."

The train rolled out toward Manhattan. It entered the subway tunnel as Steven brought the Stallion inches from the back window just above the taillight. The drafts behind the train swirled violently as the downdrafts came off the top of the train pushing his hovercraft into the tracks while the side drafts made a whirlpool of turbulence. If the Stallion were to touch the middle rail, they would both be electrocuted and then hit by the next train.

He could almost reach out and touch the window as he was within two feet of the people standing inside the car. He must have been invisible, but he had no idea what would happen if his cloaking were to stop from the bugs in his software, and he had no time to dwell on the possibilities. All he knew was he had to get through this maze and put an end to this war. He would get a short break to relax at each station as the train took on more passengers filling to capacity. He now had over fifty people within fifteen feet of him without them having any clue he was outside the window staring right at them.

He sat there hovering behind the train, waiting for it to move. When it finally pulled out of the station, he kept the Stallion within inches of the window even though the wind continued to buffet and rock him as he stayed in the backwash of the train while it gathered speed. He continued flying like he was attached to the window while people looked straight at them, thinking they were seeing the tunnel behind him on his Mylar cover. They continued this game of cat-and-mouse until they pulled into Grand Central Station, where Ranger showed him a secret series of tunnels taking them up to the Forty-Seventh Street exit flying out an abandoned service tunnel and straight up toward the East River and the United Nations Tower Plaza.

Ranger looked over at him. "Turn off your software and let them see you!"

"What? Are you crazy? It's all we have to survive."

"Have faith and turn it off. Let them see us! Let God take control of this."

"Okay, here goes."

As they openly banked into the skyscraper, the lasers began hitting the Stallion. It wasn't designed for this much energy, even though most of the firepower was still being directed at the street attack. He did just as Ranger had told him and began circling the tower, letting the lasers hit his hover at will and returned fire on the tower's firing positions. He waited for it to explode as the temperatures were shooting past critical stages. Circle after circle, the direct fire intensity increased and increased as they waited for the inevitable failure of his titanium.

Tommie Davis had his men ready inside the Queens midtown tunnel. They were part of ten teams of two-hundred-fifty each. They had to work their way into position before the morning shift change. After ten years of being chased and hunted, these men knew how to creep into positions and blend into their surroundings unseen. This exercise was different than most because the guards were on full war alert.

All the men had heard about the nuclear attack on Dallas and were ready to exact their payback or die trying. At nine o'clock, the attack

The Republic of Texas

began as two fully armored panel trucks came speeding up First Avenue, firing lasers and rockets into the compound and hitting the Secretariat Tower, causing minor explosions throughout the compound. The men cried out, "Don't mess with Texas," as they came out of their hidden positions and attacked the compound in full view.

The UN troops began the counterattack as well from the wall- and roof-mounted lasers, keeping Ranger's troops pinned down. Ranger's forces were firing from all angles on the South sector of the compound behind their armored trucks. They were combining their laser intensity on the laser mounts on the tower walls forcing the operators and spotters to keep their heads down. That's when they heard the sound they all feared the most coming up the East River. Appearing from behind the tower was another Hover Fortress with the loud whining of its powerful turbines and multiple power lasers lighting a maze of misery on the troops. It looked like a thousand-legged spider being held up by thin lights spinning a web of death.

The black Hover Fortress blocked out the sky with its immense circumference. It immediately began firing in a hundred different directions, hitting men or destroying their covered positions. It immediately took out the first armored truck while the second one was firing at the hovering monster in a futile attempt to engage it with little, if any, effect. It was putting up an impressive fight, although they knew that the ultimate outcome was going to bring about their deaths. The ground troops could all see the Black Stallion flying up the street with no camouflage and bank around the back of the tower, which reignited the spirits and caused the helpless truck to drive full speed right at the hovering Fortress.

From the north, over a thousand men swarmed down First Avenue with ten more armored trucks firing on the building and surrounding troops. They began hitting the building taking out troops stationed around it as the battle immediately was now on three sides of the compound.

Ranger yelled to Steven, "When you finish the seventh trip, you have to go inverted and give this battle to God!"

"What are you talking about? That would be instant suicide. I have almost no deflection on the bottom of my hover."

"Steven, you have to trust God completely and go inverted."

"Here goes!"

On the seventh trip around the tower, the army below blew all the brass trumpets they brought as a call out to the Lord—and then it happened. Every one of the UN lasers from all sides, as well as the Hover Fortress, hit the inverted Stallion at the same time, knocking the Stallion downward as a surge shorted the computers turning the mylar into a blinding silver mirror, reflecting the energy back into the side of the tower while the lasers intertwined, forming a nova laser, cutting the building in half. The steel girders were severed and immediately collapsed from the weight above them, beginning the pancake collapse. Everyone watched as the entire building began to tip and slowly collapsed upon itself into a giant cloud of dust engulfing half of the compound. Within minutes the entire tower was nothing more than a smoldering mountain of rubble turning into a raging pyre of paper, plastic, and wood furniture with the screams of people dying inside.

The Black Stallion spun out of control from the hit and spun into the middle of the river, bouncing numerous times before settling upright. The armored truck exploded in a giant fireball just as the tower began to collapse. The Fortress pilot never saw the collapse as it was directly behind the tail structure because a huge chunk of tower structure came crashing through the center of the massive black Fortress. This destroyed the entire engine compartment and fuel tanks, causing it to lose control as it came apart in an orange ball of fire, sending the death machine spinning out into its own watery grave.

A huge cheer came up from the troops as they began surging toward the compound and firing on anything that was moving inside the smoldering pile of debris. Within minutes, the compound guards were raising their hands to get away from the intense heat of the burning building. They could hear screams and cries coming from inside the twisted remains as the heat and flame reached into the depths of the deepest caverns and bunkers beneath the footprint where the tower just stood.

The Ranger's ground troops continued down the street toward Central Park, taking out the gangs and union troops who were running aimlessly while the Ranger's numbers swelled as they conquered block after block. The gangs lost their courage when they saw the collapse and either surrendered or ran from the vigilantes as they understood the upcoming retribution from the Christians.

Steven unbuckled his chest harness as the Black Stallion began to sink into the frigid water. The river was pouring into the gashes and damage covering the right side of the craft. He looked over at Ranger, who was unconscious, and began to shake him. "Ranger, wake up; we have to get out of here."

He began to stir, looked over at Steven, then began to comprehend the situation, looking down at his lifeless legs. "I can't get out of my harness, and my legs are trapped against the crushed metal of the hover. Can you reach over and open my harness?"

"Here, let me reach in there. It seems to be jammed, but I think if I pull this emergency release, the harness completely comes off. Okay, there we go. Grab my hand and let me help you out."

"Steven, I think the leg is rebroken and crushed. The console is completely smashed against my legs, and I think they may be broken. Unless you have a blowtorch or a Jaws of Life, I don't think I'm getting out, and this water is coming in pretty fast."

"We can get you out of here. Let me over there and see if I can free your legs."

Steven looked down Ranger's legs and could see the metal had crashed down on his thighs, and his feet were completely hidden under the crumpled metal. They tried pulling him out by lifting his shoulders and soon found it impossible to move him.

"Steven, this is the end, when your faith is really tested. I learned in prison they can take everything from me, including my dignity, but they cannot take away my faith in God. So, I may not survive this, but my faith is stronger now than it has ever been in my life. I am ready to see my family again for eternity. This will be my final baptism, and in a few moments, I will be meeting my Savior. Steven, do not ever feel bad for me or have sadness since I will be waiting for you in glory.

"Look over there at that pile of rubble, which used to be the UN. Our faith did that. Years from now, when our story is told, they will know we put our faith in God and turned off the deflectors, flew inverted to change the world. Save yourself, brother, and we will see each other again."

The Black Stallion filled completely with water and sank straight to the bottom, taking the Texas Ranger into the dark depths of the icy blackness as Steven slowly swam back to the bank. He pulled himself up on the gravel and began sobbing while he looked over at the empty flowing waters.

The wedding was being held at Ground Zero in Dallas. The reclamation crews had been working twenty-four hours a day, six days a week for the last six months, to haul the radioactive material out of the blast zone and haul in landfill, making the ground they were on completely safe. They had accomplished the impossible with help from around the world of moving over a million lead-lined truckloads of blast material and dirt out of the Dallas blast zone and were replacing it with new fill dirt twenty feet deep.

The open-air ceremony was on a stage on a newly planted grass field with new landscaping, which would become a ground zero park commemorating the over two million deaths from the nuclear attack on Dallas. The beginning of the park was starting to reveal itself and was breathtaking with the rolling hills and large reflecting pools, lakes with newly planted trees from around the world. There were already streets being laid out surrounding the park area and foundations being dug for the rebuilding of Dallas city center. The largest building would be the

The Republic of Texas

new Moses Tower II, which was being designed to be an exact copy of the Houston tower. While the Houston tower was considered the energy capital of the world, the Dallas tower was being built to become one of the world's financial capitals.

The stage overlooked the park's Ranger Memorial Lake on a perfect sunny afternoon with a crowd as far as the eye could see. A VIP section, including President Stewart, US President Victoria Price, Chinese Premier Zuan, along every major leader in the world, was set on a podium to the right of the stage. The Texas delegation, including all the senators and congressmen, was to the left. Also attending were the newly admitted sister-state representatives of Oklahoma, Louisiana, Arkansas, New Mexico, and Mississippi. It looked as if the entire Texas Christ Church of New York had traveled to be there in celebration. Pastor Darling was officiating the wedding while Jeff Drake was Steven's best man. Steven was dressed in a black tuxedo and tails with a white bow tie. Jeff was dressed in a matching tuxedo except for a bolero tie and a gold nugget slide as they made a striking image waiting for the ceremony to begin.

The entire crowd was wearing their cowboy best. The men were in cowboy boots and hats while the women were wearing the biggest dresses they could find with their Easter bonnets. Moses Industries provided a costume pavilion that had been fully stocked for anyone who did not have their own boots and hats. Even Premier Zuan was wearing his hat and boots with a cowboy-tailored suit while his wife was wearing silk flowing dress and ornate hat, which looked right out of a Western saloon.

The wedding started with the slow entrance down the boulevard of a single, completely refurbished 1890s stagecoach being pulled by six matching white stallions. The stagecoach was decorated by bouquets of flowers and multicolored mylar strips woven in the wheels. When it arrived, a half-dozen cowboys helped June Darling out of the coach as Dean Sally Sherwood, her maid of honor, helped her with her wedding gown and train. As the wedding march began, the entire crowd turned to look at the bride. She was blazingly radiant. She looked like a princess with her long, flowing gown trailing ten feet behind her and her wind-blown veil billowing down her front. She slowly made her way to the lectern, where she could see her father waiting with moistened eyes.

"Ladies and gentlemen, I have the rare opportunity to do what every father dreams of one day doing, which is marrying his own daughter to the man she loves with all her heart. Steven Moses, I have always loved my June Bug from the moment she was born and always will. I am proud to give her over to you since I know you will guard her heart, her spirit, and her mind like I have for the rest of your life."

"I promise I will, sir."

"June, it's about time!" he said, making her and the crowd laugh.

"It is about time. It is about you, June Darling, promising to give the rest of your time with Steven, and Steven Moses promising to give his name and the rest of his time with you. So, you are making this promise in front of your family, your friends, and God to spend the rest of your time devoted to each other."

"Steven, do you have the ring?"

"Yes, I do, Pastor."

"Call me dad." The crowd laughed again.

Steven reached over to Jeff, who handed him the ring. The ruby was gone, and only the large diamond was left in a silver and gold setting. June's eyes teared as she understood its meaning while looking into Steve's eyes—he nodded yes.

"Steven Moses, this ring represents the endlessness of time, which, thanks to Jesus' promise, is how long your love will last with June. Steven, do you promise to love and lead June through good times and bad, through sickness and in health, for better or for worse, forsaking all others through all the days of your life, till death do you part?"

"I do, and I will."

"June, do you promise to love and respect Steven through good times and bad, through sickness and in health, for better or for worse, forsaking all others through all the days of your life, until death do you part?"

She choked out the words as the tears flowed freely down her cheeks. "I do, and I will."

"You may kiss my daughter, your bride."

He lifted the veil to see an angelic face filled with tears of joy as he leaned her back for a wet and lingering wildcatter kiss. Not any kiss, but the kiss he had longed for, for years. A kiss he had missed since the day Sandy had died and her lips went dry; a kiss which not only made his heart stop but cleansed his entire body of the tightness, which suddenly disappeared as he became complete again. He could finally catch his breath for the first time in nearly a decade. This was a kiss to make a man look forward to the rest of his life with his woman.

June nearly fainted from the emotion she felt with his kiss. His passion and depth tore through her heart like an arrow through a hay bale. She understood the healing he felt from this moment as the past pain was washed away, and their new life began as her husband was completed, as was she.

"With the power given to me by the Republic of Texas, I now pronounce you husband and wife. May I introduce you for the first time— Mr. and Mrs. Steven Moses."

The "Yellow Rose of Texas" began playing amid emotional applause as they walked out arm in arm to the sweet smells of mesquite and hickory smoke wafting in the wind. The line dancing went on throughout the day, and even Premier Zuan and his wife were kicking up some dust in their boots and hats, whooping it up.

As the day wore on and the festivities were waning, Jeff Drake stood up and made an announcement. "Steven, we couldn't think of what to get a guy who has everything, and there was only one thing you loved nearly as much as June, and I don't mean a new oil gusher. He reached into his pocket and clicked a button. In the distance, you could see a speck growing and coming right at them and fluttering to a stop next to Steven and June. It was the Black Stallion with General Terry Thomas getting out. On the driver's doors were painted two Hover Fortresses and the United Nations building.

Jeff Drake explained the details of the craft, "We had it rebuilt from the ground up and added a bit more power for you. If you look underneath, you will see we added a ramjet booster to it in case you want to get up to Mach 6 or 7. Go easy on it at first, so you learn the power and feel at those speeds. We just want to make sure you're not shooting down any more fortresses or anything. Congratulations, Steven and June."

Steven was caught off guard and found himself a bit choked up. "I just don't know what to say! Last I saw the Stallion; it was sinking into the depths of the river with the Texas Ranger. How did you find it? How did you—? Oh well, you got me the perfect gift for a perfect day. I think this is a good time for its shakedown ride since we're taking our honeymoon down in the Caribbean. There's a special restaurant I want to stop at with June."

"Let me help you in to your carriage, my lady."

"Who said chivalry is dead?"

Steven helped June into the Black Stallion and jumped into the pilot's seat while firing it up.

Jeff yelled, "Hit the horn!"

When he hit it, it blared, "Don't mess with Texas!"

They both laughed and waved to the crowd while the applause and cheers rang out as he blasted off at full throttle and corkscrewed into the sky, then banked toward the southeast, where all the wedding guests saw the ramjet fire propelling them across the dimming sky like a shooting star streaking across the purple Texan stratosphere. Steven and June disappeared into the Texan blue yonder.

THE END

CPSIA information can be obtained
at www.ICGtesting.com
Printed in the USA
BVHW091130061122
650888BV00006B/23